INVESTMENT

Investment will always be an enterprise calling for a character which combines patience and shrewdness with a readiness to undertake some risk. For those who are prepared to exercise these qualities, having first taught themselves something about the subject and thereafter never straying too far from professional advice, investment can be a rewarding occupation in more ways than one.

Other books in the Teach Yourself series

ORIGAMI
COMPUTER PROGRAMMING
KARATE
JUDO

and available in Hodder Paperbacks

Investment

W. L. B. Fairweather, C.A.
with a foreword by
Ian Fairbairn

HODDER PAPERBACKS

© Copyright The English Universities
Press Ltd. 1960, 1970
First printed 1960
Hodder Paperback edition 1971

This book is sold subject to the condition that it shall
not, by way of trade or otherwise, be lent, re-sold,
hired out or otherwise circulated without the publisher's
prior consent in any form of binding or cover other than
that in which this is published and without a similar
condition including this condition being imposed on
the subsequent purchaser.

Printed in Great Britain
for Hodder Paperbacks, Ltd.,
St. Paul's House, Warwick Lane, London, E.C.4,
by Richard Clay (The Chaucer Press), Ltd.,
Bungay, Suffolk

ISBN 0 340 14812 8

AUTHOR'S NOTE TO SECOND EDITION: 1970

The past eighteen months have witnessed remarkable changes in the investment outlook which have emphasized once again the need for knowledge and common sense in the individual's approach to his investment problems. It is in the nature of investment to be involved, especially in times of rapid change, with the unknown almost as much as with the known. There are certainties and uncertainties and it is one of the investor's most difficult problems to be able successfully to distinguish between the two. Markets move in cycles. They always have and it is probable that they always will. For this the investor is partly responsible. As share prices rise he is apt to find their attractions irresistible. Why should he hold on to securities which he bought originally for the safety they offered when all they do is day by day fall in price? Why not follow the others who are making a great deal of money by investing in what everyone else is investing in? So he becomes interested in prices and how they move and forgets about the underlying values which prices are supposed to reflect. He is already moving on to the road which leads to ruin. In extreme cases he sells out all the securities which have brought him nothing but loss and buys only the securities whose price performance has been unexceptionably good. The market turns and falls. It has been well said in the past that markets reach their most dangerous point when all are bulls and there are no bears. At that point buying power has become exhausted and the field is wide open to the bears ready to sell what they do not have in the belief that they will be able to buy back much lower down and turn in for themselves a very good profit in the process.

The investor has a perfectly good protection against these tendencies and it is, come what may, to maintain a balanced portfolio and to change it only at the margin where he believes after due consideration that by doing this or doing that he might improve its quality without in any fundamental sense changing it. Above all he should be very wary of the investment counsellor who claims "certain" knowledge of the shape of things to come.

Two final points of a detailed character might be worth making. In spite of all that has recently happened, what has been called the "cult" of the equity remains very strong. This takes many forms. Large corporations are ready to pay $10\frac{1}{2}\%$ on money they borrow rather than issue new Ordinary shares on which they would currently have to pay no more than 5%. The justification given is the cost of corporation tax which effectively reduces the cost of $10\frac{1}{2}\%$ to a mere $5\frac{3}{4}\%$, but only if the company continues to make profits and pay tax. But is that the whole story? Will the new investment for which this money is being raised necessarily pay and is not the rate of interest proposed an unnecessarily high burden to place on the company should it ever run into conditions which threaten even its capacity to make profits? The company might have to pay 5% to its new shareholders now but it has no obligation to do so in the future should it run into more difficult times.

Another form of this "cult" is the habit of comparing "gilt-edged" yields with "equity" yields as if all investors were companies. To a company the yield on a Government stock after corporation tax has been paid is under $5\frac{1}{2}\%$ whereas to a private investor it remains $9\frac{3}{4}\%$, a consideration very much to be kept in mind.

The second point which also affects "gilt-edged" yields concerns the status of un-dated stocks. It is commonly supposed that these stocks, because they lack a final date of redemption, are very much more risky than stocks which have such a date. There is of course some truth in this but a good deal less than is generally thought. The value of a Fixed Interest stock is the present value of the income it produces during its life plus the present value of the capital sum payable on redemption, if it is a redeemable stock. The current yield on 3% Treasury Stock which has no fixed date of redemption, is $9\frac{1}{2}\%$ gross or $5\frac{5}{8}\%$ net after tax at 8s. 3d. in the £. On the assumption that £100 is invested in the stock, the present value of the interest the investor will receive over the next 19 years, which corresponds to the life of 3% Transport Stock 1978-88, assuming that he wants a clear $5\frac{1}{2}\%$ net on his investment, will be £65. This means that of the sum of £100 he lays down, he is paying

£65 for an annuity certain for 19 years and only £35 for the annuity which will continue for the rest of time thereafter unless, owing to a very sharp fall in interest rates, the stock is redeemed at par. In that event he will have reaped a very handsome capital profit of the order of 200% on his original purchase price.

TO MY WIFE

ACKNOWLEDGEMENTS

The author wishes to thank Mr. Ian Fairbairn for the great help he has given during the preparation of this work. He has guided the author through the difficult formative stages and assisted him later by giving freely of his time, his hospitality and his wide knowledge and experience of the subjects discussed. His aim throughout was however to prompt rather than to direct, and if as the result the book that has emerged is one to which he feels able to give his approval, this is in no small measure due to the creative part which he himself has played.

The author also wishes to thank Mr. Paul Bareau for reading through and commenting on the economic sections of the book, Mr. R. S. Caverhill, F.I.A., for his help on the sections dealing with Life Assurance and Pensions, Mr. G. T. Wickes for his guidance on the functions of jobbers, Mr. J. H. Lane Fox, M.A., F.R.I.C., for his advice on the problems of Real Property Investment, Mr. Guy Libby and Major H. F. Otway, M.C., for information they provided on Trusts and Mr. G. H. Whitehall for his assistance on recent changes in Stock Exchange procedure and other matters.

The author finally wishes to thank The Delta Metal Company Limited for agreeing to the use of their 1957 published Accounts to illustrate a Balance Sheet and Profit and Loss Account and the Misses L. and R. Bullock for their help in preparing the drafts and final manuscript.

FOREWORD
By Ian Fairbairn

Investment is not a difficult subject for anybody wishing to get an amateur's broad understanding of the whole matter and some detailed appreciation of the most important component parts. In any capitalist country, moreover, it is of great practical importance to many people. And yet a surprisingly large proportion of such people, in this country at least, are sadly ignorant of the whole subject. Literally, sadly ignorant: they are depressingly aware of their ignorance, for they realize that it is dangerous for them to be ignorant on this subject, and yet they are at a loss to know how to remedy their ignorance. That goes for many professional men and women, to be found in the ranks of the Civil Service for instance, the armed forces, and indeed amongst all sorts and conditions of educated folk. Clergymen, in the days when they had a little capital, were notoriously the prey of the sharepusher. Recently we have seen Church dignitaries, who were concerned to administer ecclesiastical funds, suffering quite unnecessary mental turmoil as a result of their ignorance of what is the fundamental difference between the virtues of investment and the vices of gambling.

In my opinion, none of these people would be wise to attempt to look after their investment affairs by themselves; they should get good professional advice, which in investment matters as in others is about the most valuable thing one can have. But that is not to say that the investor had better not understand or try to appreciate what is behind the advice he will be given; nor is it to say that he can easily find his way to good advice and keep a check on the quality of that advice (when, for example, the personnel of a firm changes), unless he has some broad understanding of investment and its many difficulties.

Reading Mr. Fairweather's book should enable anybody who has the responsibility of owning capital to know how to set about making the best use of it, to feel that he (or she) is discharging that responsibility in the best interests of himself, his family and the community, to feel assured that he is handling his affairs competently. It will also enlighten savers who are beginning to build up capital. It will help both those who already have capital and those who are putting savings by to take a vastly wider and more satisfying interest in investment than the mere observation of changes in prices of securities and in dividends. The reader will get an understanding of the useful, indeed vital, part played by the investor in a free community. He will find here a lucid and badly needed simple exposition of the various effects of inflation on different kinds of investment, and I would guess that most readers will acquire a much clearer understanding than they had before of that evil, which has replaced unemployment as the canker of our free-enterprise society. For this reason I could wish that the book will be widely read amongst our politicians and those who influence them.

It is perhaps not too optimistic to hope that this book may encourage some, who up to now had not contemplated doing so, to venture into the wide fields of capital enterprise by joining the ranks of those who through their investment own our commercial and industrial undertakings. There has already been something of a social revolution in this respect during the last few decades, and there is a widespread hope that it will go much further. Not so long ago investment in stocks and shares in this country was something which, practically speaking, fell into the category of class distinction. It would have seemed unnatural—and above his station—for a gamekeeper or a domestic servant to own shares; and, more strangely perhaps, ladies of whatever rank or wealth were not supposed to invest outside the respectability of "The Funds" —well, perhaps a little in the best railway stocks, God save the mark! This misconceived convention was prevalent when I first knew the City forty years ago: certain investments were considered very good for eminent City people and even for myself, but quite unsuitable for ladies. "Now, if you want a really interesting investment," I would be told by some kindly City magnate, "for yourself mind you, not for the widow or orphan . . ." It was puzzling to be told that such investments could be good for my intelligent and experienced elderly friends and for myself but bad for widows and orphans. I confirmed by experience that on the whole they were good for me; and an irrepressible sense of logic drove me to believe that they ought to be good for widows and orphans, a conclusion which actual experiences again have demonstrated to be true. Today few will be found to deny that in investment opportunity all men and women should be free and equal.

The delusion that an investment could be good for City magnates but not for widows and orphans probably arose from two related Victorian conventional ideas. These were the idea that certain investments offered complete security in perpetuity, and the idea that any other investment was more or less speculative and therefore more or less morally questionable; and in those days, it must be remembered, there was sharper distinction than today between what was permitted to men and what to women by way of trespass or adventure into any activity or behaviour which was at all questionable.

Some may still think that there ought to be investments which offer complete security in perpetuity. Perhaps governments ought never to default on their obligations, and perhaps they ought to be wise and honest enough to maintain the value of the national currency, while at the same time avoiding sharp movements in interest rates. Our Victorian governments were by and large so successful in those respects that one can understand how the idea of the cast-iron security of "The Funds" grew up. But as we survey investments more than half a century later and after two world-shaking wars the scene is very different. Nor do I think, if I may wander for a moment into the Victorian's field of moralizing, that cast-iron security is what is intended by Providence for mortal investors. If only Adam had not got himself, and therefore us his sons and daughters, excluded from Paradise, cast-iron security there would have been for all, even without investment. But ever since that lapse man's lot has been to live by the sweat of his brow; and not least is the sweat of looking after investments amidst the changes and chances of this mortal life. Although I am wholly incompetent to expound the Gospel, I may perhaps be permitted to add that in the parable of the talents I find nothing to encourage me to eschew speculation and to play for cast-iron safety.

That brings us to the other idea, the idea that speculation

is different from investment, and more or less disreputable. "Speculate" is one of those words which have come down in the world, like the closely related "adventurer": it certainly has today for most people in most contexts some implication of abandoning the morally and economically correct hard high roads of investment for the softer and more devious primrose paths of chance. And yet its dictionary definition gives no such implication: "(1) Pursue an inquiry, meditate, form theory or conjectural opinion . . . (2) Make investment, engage in commercial operation, that involves risk of loss . . ." (C.O.D.). It seems obvious that all investment must involve speculation in the sense that the investor should always rack his brains about the prospects of any investment he may contemplate making—"pursue an inquiry" about it, and "meditate"—before acting. As for an "investment . . . that involves risk of loss", I should like to know of one that does not, as would no doubt many an investor who put his money into Consols in years gone by, carefree in the delusion that "The Funds" were risk-proof, to say nothing of highly respectable German old ladies who starved—literally, starved to death—with their Prussian 3% stock in the inflation of the 1920's. What has happened is that "speculate" has become confused in people's minds with "gamble", which is defined in the C.O.D. as "Play games of chance for money . . ." Some element of chance there is likely to be in all investment, deriving from the unforeseen and unforeseeable. But the job of the investor is to eliminate chance as much as possible by speculation, by pursuing all relevant inquiry and by meditating on what he thereby uncovers. The result though offering nothing like a cast-iron certainty is something very different from blind chance, which decides the spin of a coin, the turn of Fortune's wheel or even Ernie.

Investment will always be an enterprise calling for a character which combines patience and shrewdness with a readiness to undertake some risk. For those who are prepared to exercise these qualities, having first taught themselves something about the subject and thereafter never straying too far from professional advice, investment can be a rewarding occupation in more ways than one.

CONTENTS

PART I: THE NATURE OF INVESTMENT

I SAVING AND INVESTMENT . . . 1
Investment and its connection with Consumption and Saving—Inflation and Deflation—The Field of Government Action—New Saving and Investment—The Finance of Investment—The Importance of the Saver.

II TYPES OF PRIVATE INVESTMENT . . 14
Introductory—Life Assurance—Pensions—National Savings—Building Society Deposits and Shares and Bank Deposits—Real Property—Property Mortgages and other Secured and Unsecured Private Loans—Marketable Securities.

PART II: MARKETABLE SECURITIES

III THE RANGE AND MARKET OF MARKETABLE SECURITIES 27
The Range of Securities—Dealing in Marketable Securities—Income—Information—Summary.

IV GENERAL INFLUENCES AFFECTING PRICES OF MARKETABLE SECURITIES 36
Yield—The Rate of Interest—How the Rate of Interest is decided—The Balance of Payments—General Economic Conditions—Inflation—Politics.

V FIXED INTEREST SECURITIES—GENERAL . . 47
Description—Yields on Redeemable Securities—Redeemable and Irredeemable Securities Compared—The Quality of Securities.

CONTENTS

VI CLASSES OF FIXED INTEREST SECURITIES . . 55
The Range—British Government Securities—Commonwealth and Colonial Government Securities—Local Authority Stocks—Public Boards and the Stocks of Water Works Companies—Loans and Debenture Stocks of Commercial and Industrial Companies—Preference Stocks—Foreign Bonds.

VII ORDINARY SHARES AND STOCKS—GENERAL . . 66
Description—The Raising of New Capital—Reading Company Accounts—Yields.

VIII BRITISH ORDINARY SHARES AND STOCKS . . 78
The Effects of Post-War Inflation—The Value of Ordinary Shares—Types of British Ordinary Shares.

IX THE ORDINARY SHARES AND COMMON STOCKS OF OTHER COUNTRIES 91
Foreign Shares and Stocks—Commonwealth and South African Shares and Stocks.

X INVESTMENT TRUST COMPANIES AND UNIT TRUSTS 101
General — Investment Companies — Unit Trusts.

PART III: INVESTMENT POLICY

XI THE NEED FOR AN ACTIVE INVESTMENT POLICY . 111
The Importance of Good Timing—The Rate of Interest and Security Prices—Ordinary Dividend Income—Forecasting the Rate of Interest—Conclusion.

XII THE GENERAL INVESTMENT BACKGROUND . . 122
Inflation is antagonistic to the interests of the Investor—The End of Inflation may be in Sight.

CONTENTS

XIII THE NEED FOR INVESTMENT SPREAD . . . 131
  Should Fixed Interest Securities be included?
  —Ordinary Shares must be included and they
  should be well spread.

PART IV: HOW TO SELECT SECURITIES

XIV TAXATION AND THE INVESTOR 139
  Income Tax and Yields—Company Taxes—
  Tax on Capital Gains—Tax and Cum and Ex
  Dealings.

XV THE CHOICE OF INDIVIDUAL SECURITIES . 147
  The Investment Background: The Country
  —The Industry—The Record of the Company
  —Financial Strength—Yield—Market Considerations—Fixed Interest Securities.

XVI THE PROFESSION OF INVESTMENT ADVISING . 157
  Advising the Investor—The Pursuit of Profits
  —Where the Investor should go for Advice.

APPENDICES

I Index to the Stock Exchange Daily Official List 162
II Buying and Selling Contract Notes . . 163
III Official Scale of Minimum Commissions . 165
IV How to Calculate Yields 167
V Government Control of Interest Rates . 170
VI Yields on Redeemable Securities . . . 173
VII Sample Balance Sheet 174
VIII Sample Profit and Loss Account . . 177
  Index 181

PART I THE NATURE OF INVESTMENT

CHAPTER I

SAVING AND INVESTMENT

Investment and its connection with Consumption and Saving

The object of investment is the increase of income. This is as true of the housewife who installs a washing machine in order to save her energy or cut down her laundry bills as it is of the industrialist who erects a plant to meet a new need or to reduce his labour costs. In each case there is an increase of income or of well-being (which is the same thing), the release of energy for a new creative task or for leisure or the satisfaction of a new need. The average house of today is a very different affair from the average house of a hundred years ago. The difference is represented very largely by an investment in plumbing. The investment may appear to yield no income to those who own and live in the house. But it has an income value none the less in the greater comfort and convenience of living in a well-equipped modern house, just as it has a commercial value the moment the house is put on the market for sale.

The income from an investment depends ultimately on the investment's ability to serve a consumer's need, whether it be a washing machine, a house or a factory. A factory, for example, is erected not because the factory has any value in itself but because the owner hopes to make an income out of it by producing goods which the consumer wants, or which will help other producers to produce goods which the consumer wants. At the end of the road always is the consumer who decides finally whether or not the investment has been worthwhile.

As it is true that the value of an investment ultimately depends upon the needs and wishes of the consumer, so it is true that an investment cannot come into being without an equal amount of saving. While people are building factories and receiving incomes for building them, they cannot be making the consumers goods on which for the most part they will want to spend their incomes. Therefore they and the makers of consumers goods must between them save enough of their incomes to pay for the building of the factory. The operative word is must. They may not initially want to save so much. For their service as producers they are paid in money which they are free to spend on consumption or save as they please. They may divide their incomes between spending and saving in the same proportions as their joint output has been divided between consumption goods and investment goods, but there is no law which makes them automatically do so. If they spend too much of their incomes on consumption, there will not be enough consumers goods to meet all their demands unless prices are raised. In that event, the owners of the goods —the employer producers, or entrepreneurs as economists call them, will make exceptional profits. These profits, if saved, will replace the undersaving which gave rise to them and if not saved, will generate further price rises and further exceptional profits. The saving, in other words, which was not made initially will be transferred to others through the operation of rising prices.

If conversely people save too much of their income, i.e. spend too little, entrepreneurs will be left with larger stocks of consumption goods on their hands than they anticipated. To dispose of them, they may have to lower their selling prices, reducing their profits in the process. Faced with lower profits and therefore lower incomes for themselves, they may either reduce their own saving, thereby offsetting the extra saving of other people, or they may reduce their own consumption. In the latter event the problem of too much saving will remain, leading to further price reductions and further profit contractions, until the excessive savings of the public are neutralized by reduced savings of entrepreneurs.

Inflation and Deflation

It will be useful to follow these illustrations a little further because they describe the two conditions known to economists and governments as inflation and deflation.

In the first illustration, consumption has risen, prices have risen and profits have risen. Investment has remained unchanged and the reduced savings of people in general have been matched by increased savings of entrepreneurs. Now as we said earlier, the value of investment depends ultimately on consumption. The consumer has shown that he wants more. Therefore the entrepreneur, as it will be in his own interest to do so, will want to give him more. To do so, however, he may have to build a new factory.

Let us suppose that the extra profits he is making provide him with just enough money to pay for the new factory. Soon he finds he has another worry. He cannot find the people to build his factory. After a good deal of trouble, he gets over this difficulty by paying more for his factory than he intended, thereby making it possible for higher wages to be paid to building workers. Some of these workers may previously have been doing other kinds of building work. In that event, the investment in the new factory will be achieved partly at the expense of other kinds of investment. But some of them may also have been engaged previously in making consumption goods. In that event, the new factory will be built partly at the expense of a reduced output of consumption goods.

As a manufacturer of consumers goods himself he will not want to lose any of his existing labour force. On the other hand, other manufacturers with factory capacity to spare will want to engage more workpeople. The result will be a tug of war in which neither consumption nor investment will gain. They may indeed suffer as the result of production dislocations and the extra initiative that will have to be put into the search for scarce resources. The prices of everything will rise, however, and there will be a general redistribution of incomes in favour of the owners of goods and property and of those who are in a strong enough bargaining position to get wage and salary increases.

This is the condition of inflation. It is likely to occur only where existing resources, chiefly labour, are already fully committed in the service of consumption and investment and where people increase their demand for consumption goods and there is no compensating reduction in the demand for investment goods or where there is an increased demand for investment goods without a compensating reduction in the demand for consumption goods. The latter can happen where the main stimulus to new investment is coming from an increased demand for consumption goods. It can also happen where a new invention has created new opportunities for investment.

If at the time when people decide to spend more on consumption goods there are idle resources waiting to be absorbed into production, then it should be possible to build the new factory, without putting up the price of labour and to increase the output of consumers goods, by drawing unemployed workpeople into the factories which have idle capacity to spare. In that situation, the rise in the demand for consumption goods will be wholly beneficial in its effects. Production will rise, incomes will rise, investment (the new factory) will rise and saving (the ownership of the new factory) will rise and all with the minimum disturbance to prices.

In the second illustration, consumption has fallen, prices have fallen and profits have fallen. In this situation, entrepreneurs will not want to spend money on new factories to make goods which are already being made in more than adequate quantities by existing factories. Rather will they want to curtail any plans they may have had for developments of that kind. At the same time they will want to reduce their output of consumers goods so as to avoid an undue rise in the stocks they normally carry. As they reduce output, incomes will be reduced. People will then have less absolutely to spend on consumption goods. In this situation with their jobs threatened they may decide to save even more. This will further aggravate the situation, bringing further cuts in production and incomes and in time, if the movement goes far enough, investment production may come almost completely to a standstill. The process of deflation will be complete and an economic depression or slump will have arrived.

The Field of Government Action

It requires no special insight to deduce from these illustrations that inflation and deflation are both conditions to be avoided and that the ideal state is one where the demands on resources both for consumption and investment balance approximately with the supply, in such a way as to avoid an

SAVING AND INVESTMENT

upward spiral of wages and prices on the one hand and a falling level of production and incomes on the other. Provided these general conditions can be assured, the individual working for his own advantage should also be working for society's advantage, for there will be enough demand to encourage him to make the maximum use of existing resources, knowledge and inventiveness for his own profit and enough competition to ensure that the extra product created will be shared with his workpeople and with consumers.

It should also require no special insight to appreciate that the attainment of this balance is not something that happens of its own accord. It does not; and when the balance goes wrong either in the direction of inflation or of deflation, there are natural forces in the urge to increase profits or to limit losses, that make it go further wrong. When there is inflation, people are inclined to spend more not less, because they expect prices tomorrow to be higher than they are today. When there is deflation, people want to spend less not more, for the opposite reason, that prices tomorrow are likely to be less than they are today.

Fortunately it is now recognized that the Government has a duty to intervene, and for this purpose it has two powerful weapons, the general control it exercises, through the Bank of England, over interest rates and the supply of money and its power, through the Budget, to increase or reduce the amount of income at the disposal of people. Through its general control over the supply of money it can increase or reduce the supply of money available to investors. In this way it can make it easier or more difficult, as the case might be, for them to go ahead with projects which they have under consideration. If it increases the supply of money, it will tend to lower the rate of interest which borrowers have to pay and in this way make it less expensive for business men to raise money for their projects. Conversely if it reduces the supply of money, it will tend to raise the rate of interest which borrowers have to pay and in this way make it more expensive for business men to borrow. As business men will ultimately decide whether or not to go ahead with their projects by reference to the income they expect from them, variations in the costs of borrowing may decisively affect their plans.

The Government's control over the situation through the Budget is more direct although slower in action. The Government can spend more than it takes back from the public in taxes—a Budget deficit; or it can spend less than it takes back from the public in taxes—a Budget surplus. In this way it can increase or reduce the incomes available to the public and therefore their spending power. The weapon is at present less highly developed than the monetary weapon but it is one of which more and more use may be made as knowledge and experience grow.

These are matters to which we will return later because of their important bearing on investment problems generally. For the present we shall merely note that a state of gathering inflation implies early action by the Government to raise interest rates and to increase taxes or reduce spendings, and that the threat of deflation implies early action of the opposite kind.

New Saving and Investment

Each year the Government makes estimates of the nation's total savings during the previous calendar year and the total investment that has been financed by means of this saving. The figures are expressed gross. That is to say they show the total amounts that individuals, companies, the Government and Local Authorities have saved out of their income each year, but make insufficient allowance for the using up of past savings that is constantly taking place. In the same way they show the total amount that has been spent each year on factories, machinery, houses, ships, and aircraft and all manner of other investment goods, without taking account of the extent to which these expenditures merely replace old investment goods which have become worn out by age, or which have lost their worth by virtue of the invention of new and better methods of doing jobs. This makes the figures slightly unreal. A true picture of the saving and investment that has taken place in any one year would show only the value of the net additions to saving and investment in that year after full provision has been made for the using up of savings and investments carried forward from previous years. The Government meets part of this gap in knowledge by publishing each year estimates of the annual wastage of assets, i.e. of investments, but it does not show how this wastage has been shared by savers. The 1957 estimates were:

Estimate of Annual Wastage of Assets

	£ million
Vehicles, Ships and Aircraft	359
Plant and Machinery	708
Dwellings	268
Other Buildings	439
	£1,774

Another reservation about the figures is worth mentioning. They take no account, either on the savings side or on the investment side, of capital profits or capital losses. To take a simple example, if a man built a house for himself at a cost of £5,000 and subsequently decided to sell it for £7,000, the house would appear on the investment side of the national accounts at the figure of £5,000. The £2,000 capital profit he had made would not appear. Nor would it appear on the savings side even if he had saved the whole amount of it. The exclusion in this way of capital profits and losses from the accounts is defensible on the grounds that they do not represent genuine additions to current saving or investment but rather fortuitous changes in the value of savings and investment, as likely to affect the value of investments made many years earlier, as the value of investments made in the year under review. Their existence can however have considerable economic consequences in supplementing spending power, when capital profits are general and subtracting from spending power, when capital losses are general. For this reason it would be useful if more information could be made available about them; but that is by the way.

The Government's estimates of Gross National Saving and Gross National Investment in 1957 are shown on page 8.

They show that collectively individuals, companies, Public Corporations and Local Authorities saved enough out of their incomes to pay for the entire cost of the new investment that was brought into being, including additions to stocks and amounts invested abroad. They do not on the other hand

Gross National Savings		Gross National Investment	
	£ million		£ million
Personal Saving	1,484	Vehicles, Ships, Aircraft	536
Company Saving and the Saving of Public Corporations	1,926	Plant and Machinery	1,258
		Dwellings	619
Government Saving	540	Other new Buildings and Works	989
Local Authority Saving	139	Additions to Stocks	450
		Foreign Investment	237
	£4,089		£4,089

tell us anything about how this was achieved—whether 1957 was a year of inflation or of deflation, i.e. whether the balance between saving and investment was brought about through price rises and profit increases, or through price cuts and profit reductions. For that information we would need to consult the statistics of prices and employment. From them we learn that 1957, like other post-war years, was a year of inflation.

The Finance of Investment

Business men need money to finance their investment projects. They may have the money themselves but as often as not they will have to raise it from another source. In deciding whether to go ahead with their project, they will have to take this into account and also what they will have to pay for the use of money they borrow. If the rate of interest asked is too high, their ability to go ahead with the project will be impaired. On the other hand they will be ready to offer a rate of interest which they have every reason to hope they will be able to recoup from the profits of the project, or which, if it is a house they are building, compares favourably with the rent they will have to pay for the use of a similar property.

It is savers who provide money. Their concern is with the amount of income they can earn on their savings. They also invest, but unlike the investors we have up till now been discussing—not necessarily in new projects. The moment they have savings to invest, they are confronted with a wide choice of investments old and new. They may invest in the new house that is being built. That is what in effect they will do, if they lend their money to a building society which is helping house builders to build their own houses. But they may also invest in a security that has existed for many years—a Government security or the stock of one of the well-known old-established Public Companies. In that event they will not be helping directly to solve the financial problems of the new investor. Their savings, or rather the money which their savings represent, will not however disappear. It will now pass into the hands of the old investor who sold the stock and who will now have to decide what he is to do with it—whether he is to buy another old investment or whether he is to invest in some entirely new project.

The business man has, in fact, if he is to succeed in raising all the money he needs for his project, to offer terms which makes the new investment he is creating, fully as attractive as any existing investment. He may do this by offering shares in the future profits he hopes to make or he may offer a particularly attractive rate of interest for a loan secured on the entire assets of his business. How much or how little he will have to pay in terms of a share of profits or alternatively of interest on borrowed money, will depend on the prevailing rate of interest, which as we explained earlier the Government can influence, and on his own business reputation and financial standing. If the prevailing rate of interest is high (i.e. if the amount of income which money can hope to earn if invested in existing securities is high), then he will find the raising of money expensive, however good his financial standing or his reputation as a man of business may be. Equally if little is known of his ability as a man of business and his financial standing is considered at best doubtful, he may either fail to raise the money he needs or alternatively have to pay an exceptional price in interest, or in a share of his profits, for the accommodation he requires. The converse will apply, if the prevailing rate of interest is low or his ability as a man of business and his financial standing are rated high.

In the society in which we live a great deal of the country's new investment is undertaken by large public companies. These public companies finance a good deal of the cost of their new investment out of their own profits. In their origins they were mostly small private businesses which have grown over the years into vast undertakings. In the eyes of the law they are separate legal persons but in practice they are owned by hundreds and perhaps thousands of shareholders large and small. Their shares may be brought by anyone who is prepared to pay the ruling price for them. They became public, either because the original proprietors no longer felt able to shoulder the full financial responsibilities of ownership, or because their growth required more capital than the original owners were in a position to provide. And the process by which they became public was the sale of the ownership, or part of the ownership, to the public—in fact to the savers we have been discussing.

As savers are of many kinds, companies when inviting their financial interest have devised modes of investment suitable to each taste, the Loan or Debenture stock to provide the greatest safety of income, the Preference stock to provide a higher income but with less absolute safety of regular payment and the Ordinary share or stock to provide all the opportunities of ownership together with their risks.

Stocks of a company once they are issued to the public are with a few exceptions repayable only in the event of the liquidation of the company. The exceptions are Loan and Debenture stocks, where provision may be made for their repayment after a specified number of years, and Redeemable Preference stocks. Consequently if an investor (and this applies to Redeemable Debenture and Preference stocks, where they have still a period to run before their redemption dates, as well as to the other stocks) wants to realize his stocks, he must find someone else who is prepared to buy them. Then what he will receive will depend, not on what he paid for the stocks but on what the new buyer is prepared to pay for them. This may be more and may be less than he originally paid.

It follows from this that once a company issues its stocks to the public, it has no further financial interest in them, whether they rise or fall in price. The whole of the advantage or disadvantage arising from subsequent price changes accrues to the existing holders. It follows also that a rise in the price of a company's stock puts no additional money at the disposal of the company for the finance of new investment it may be contemplating, although it will help the company indirectly by making it easier for it to raise capital in the future should it wish to do so.

The Importance of the Saver

The saver directly or indirectly is the instrument by which all new investment is financed but his importance should not on that account be exaggerated. He is not, as we have seen, the promoter of new investment. The promoters of new investment are the enterprising individuals, the business men or entrepreneurs and the economic climate in which they have to work. The ideal economic climate for them exists where the demand for consumption goods is rising. The same climate may not however be favourable to the saver who has to provide both the market for consumption goods and, by abstaining from consumption, also the savings. For him an intricate balancing exercise has to be performed which, as one of a miscellaneous collection of individual savers, he has not the information to perform satisfactorily. If he saves too much he may set up deflationary forces in the economy discouraging to business men; if he saves too little, inflationary forces may result which waste resources, unsettle the value of money and cause hardships, especially to past savers who, having invested their money apparently safely, find that it is steadily losing its value.

The only agent which can ensure the right climate for the savers and the investors to do their jobs satisfactorily is the Government. Its job is to produce an economic climate in which savings and investment will grow without the aid of rising prices and on the basis of the fullest employment of the nation's material and manpower resources.

Given that, the prime mover of economic events is the business man. He decides the shape of future capital investment, the industries that are to be developed, the inventions that are to be exploited and in a large degree the economic well-being of the society in which people are to live. And his inseparable companion in all this, often at a very distant remove, is the saver, private, public and corporate. It would be possible to dispense with the private saver and the private investor by substituting the State—the Russians have done it —but whether the State by itself could ever achieve the astonishing advances in economic welfare which private capitalism has achieved during its short history, is doubtful. The economic gains of Soviet Communism over the past forty years have been considerable. But before we rush to conclusions about the advantages of State Socialism we should first be clear on the following things. First, the Russians started from a foundation of very primitive Capitalist development. Secondly, their achievements have been costly in terms of individual freedom. Thirdly, and most significantly, they have modelled their development very largely on the achievements of Capitalism and in the light of the knowledge made available by Capitalism. In the lead, would they have been capable of the advances which Capitalism has made and continues to make? The history of Capitalism is very largely the history of exceptional men whom many of their contemporaries thought odd—Watt, Arkwright, Stephenson, Bell, Ford and Marconi. But for the opportunities these men had of developing and demonstrating their own ideas, would progress have been as rapid as it has been? Indeed might it not have been frustrated at the outset because of the challenge their ideas often represented to the established order of things? A society which puts order first and last and knows already the answers to most questions or the methods by which the answers are to be found, runs the great danger of starving all its creative geniuses. Fourthly, in spite of the great economic strides that the Russians have undoubtedly made, the stage of development that they have reached is still well below the best that Capitalism has achieved.

So long as these questions remain unresolved, as they certainly remain unresolved at the present time, the case against private Capitalism is unproved and the case for it difficult to challenge. Meanwhile its structure continues to be improved and, because it is flexible, will go on being improved. Its essential feature must however be preserved—the freedom of individuals to exploit their talents and resources for their own and for society's advantage. Recurrent trade cycles gave rise in the past to questions about the adequacy of the system as a producer and distributor of wealth: but the growth of economic knowledge has found ways round this difficulty and will no doubt find ways round any other difficulties that may arise in the future, to challenge its basic soundness. Whether State Socialism, held together by an external force, will be as able to meet future challenges as and when they arise, as private Capitalism has proved itself to be, remains very much an open question.

CHAPTER II

TYPES OF PRIVATE INVESTMENT

Introductory

The saver, and especially the private saver—the ordinary man or woman—is not, as we have seen, primarily concerned with the promotion of new investment. His anxiety is to get the best possible return from the money he has available for investment. Whether he gets it from a new investment or an old investment is immaterial to him. Usually he will put his money in an old investment, leaving experts better fitted for the job than himself to handle the problem of financing new investment. The various ways in which he will normally invest his savings are as follows:

Life Assurance

The Life Assurance Policy and the Life Annuity are both types of Investment although their methods and objects are very different. In the simplest form of life Assurance Policy, i.e. whole life assurance against death, the investor effects a policy with an Insurance office, which undertakes to provide a fixed sum assured on his death, in consideration of the payment to them of a fixed annual amount, known as the premium. The rate of premium is dependent on the investor's age at entry. In so far as the premium is paid out of saved income, such a policy is a form of capital accumulation which can provide a substantial sum for the policy-holder's dependents in the event of his death. Compared to the outlay in premiums, the financial return will be high in the event of his death in the early years, but less so with each year, as further premiums are paid. The high measure of protection enjoyed by his dependents in the event of his early death has to be paid for by someone, and that someone is the more fortunate policyholder who enjoys a greater length of life, and consequently pays more premiums.

The aim of the investor in Life Annuities is by contrast not to accumulate capital but to obtain, according to his needs, the

TYPES OF PRIVATE INVESTMENT 15

maximum use of his capital during his lifetime. As the result, his capital may in the end either be entirely used up or be greatly reduced. Life Annuities have attractions to people of small means whose resources are insufficient to provide them with an adequate annual income without encroaching upon some part of their capital. They also have advantages for rich elderly persons when combined with Life Assurance Policies taken out under the Married Women's Property Acts of England and Scotland. Under these Acts, husbands or wives may take out Life Assurance Policies in favour of each other or of their children. The sums payable on death under these Policies become separate estates for Estate Duty purposes on which duty payable, not at the rates applicable to the larger estate of the deceased but at the lower rates applicable to the smaller separate estates. By combining Life Annuities and Life Assurance Policies in this way it is possible to increase the income of the insured person considerably during his or her life and at the same time achieve large Estate Duty savings on death.

The Life Assurance Policy is probably the first investment that the prudent man without capital makes. Facing life as a young man he knows that there is every likelihood that he will, as he lives, accumulate responsibilities—first towards a wife and subsequently towards his children. He will expect to remain the breadwinner, with the result that if he dies prematurely, leaving a wife and family, serious hardship will be involved for them, unless he has made provision in advance against this possibility. Yet he will know that he is unlikely in the early years of his working life to be able to save enough out of his income to make sufficient provision by accumulation in the ordinary way. The Life Assurance Policy solves this problem for him. Under a whole life policy he contracts to pay a fixed annual sum for life in return for a certain sum on death however soon or late it may occur. Thus, for example, if he lives for less than a year and has paid only one annual premium, there will be available for his dependents the same sum assured as would have been provided had he lived a normally full life and paid, say, 40 premiums.

The Inland Revenue grants relief of Income Tax on most Life Assurance premiums. Subject to the premiums not exceeding 7% of the sum assured and to them not absorbing more than one-sixth of the taxpayer's income, relief is allowed on two-fifths of the premiums paid, except that when the total annual premium is under £25, relief is allowed in the full amount of the premium or on £10, whichever is the smaller.

Such policies may be of two kinds—"non-profits" policies or "with profits" policies. "Non-profits" policies provide a fixed sum assured which does not vary during the currency of the policy, no matter how many premiums have been paid. "With profits" policies, on the other hand, provide for a fixed basic sum assured, which, it can be expected, will be augmented from year to year in respect of each premium paid, by a participation in the profits of the Assurance office. The original sum assured will be fixed at a lower figure than would apply, if the policy was a "non-profits" one, but periodically, the Assurance office will declare a bonus out of its profits, which as each premium is paid, is added to the amount payable under the policy, in the event of a claim arising thereunder.

So we see that "non-profits" policies provide a higher initial assurance cover for each £1 of premium, where death occurs in the early years of the currency of the policy. If, however, life is prolonged, the "with profits" policies may be expected through the addition of periodical bonuses to provide eventually a larger amount payable. The advantage may also be expected to lie with "with profits" policies under conditions of inflation, when as a result of rising profits the assured person may be able to obtain some offset against the diminishing value in real terms of the proceeds when received. Many "non-profits" policies taken out twenty or more years ago, for sums which then looked adequate, have a very different appearance today owing to the fall in the value of money which has occurred in the meanwhile. While "with profits" policies taken out at the same time have not fully offset the effects of the fall in the value of money, they have made a better showing. Another influence which has favoured the "with profits" policy has been the lengthening lives of people, thanks to advances in medical skill.

Apart from these main types of Life Assurance Policies the Insurance companies have devised many variations to meet different kinds of needs. The commonest variation is the Endowment Assurance Policy which provides for the payment of a capital sum on the assured person reaching a certain age or on his death if it occurs earlier. Such policies can be adapted to provide lump sums for children's education, mortgage repayment, old age or retirement, etc.

Pensions

Although the practice of providing pensions for ageing employees is growing rapidly, it is by no means yet universal. As the result many people faced with retirement are obliged to rely on the National Insurance pension, if they have been contributors, and on what they have been able to save out of their incomes during their working lives. The National Insurance pension is at present £8 2s. per week for married couples (£10 per week if both husband and wife have contributed) and £5 per week for single persons; it is payable at the age of 65 for males and 60 for females. It is widely recognized however that it does no more than attempt to provide the basic requirements of living and that in the majority of cases it must be supplemented in other ways. The pension provisions of the Finance Act of 1956 offers help to the individual who must provide largely for his own retirement. They enable him, subject to certain limitations, to deduct from his taxable earned income, the full amount of any premium he pays to an Insurance company for the purpose of buying a retirement pension. The effect of this is to reduce the actual cost of the premium or premiums he pays by the amount of income tax or surtax he saves. Because premiums so paid operate to reduce the amount of income which ranks for earned income relief, the advantage of this form of saving for retirement over other forms was partially reduced by the extension in the 1957 Finance Act of earned income relief to incomes well beyond the £2,000 range. The relative advantage has been further reduced as the result of the surtax concessions in respect of earned incomes in the 1961 Finance Act. The following is a brief summary of the provisions.

(1) Full exemption from income and surtax may be claimed in respect of any premium paid, subject to a maximum of £750 per annum or 10% of the taxpayer's earned income,

whichever is the less, if he was born in 1916 or later, or £1,125 or 15% of his earned income if he was born in 1907 or earlier. For those born during the intervening years, the allowance rises by £75 or 1% of the taxpayer's earned income, with each two years' increase in age.

(2) Where in any one year the assured person is unable, owing to a fall in his income, to claim full income and surtax exemption in respect of the premium he has paid, he may carry forward the balance of the premium to subsequent years.

(3) Pensions may begin at any time, at the option of the assured person, between the ages of 60 and 70 or in certain circumstances earlier.

(4) Pensions when paid will be assessed to tax as earned income.

(5) Policies may not be surrendered for cash nor assigned nor used as security for loans. In the event of death before the pensionable age is reached, premiums will be returned in full with or without interest, depending on the terms of the policy. Sums so returned will be exempt from income tax and surtax but will be subject to estate duty at the deceased's appropriate rate.

The arrangements have undoubtedly great attractions for those obliged to provide for their own retirement and earning large incomes subject to high rates of tax. It was however perhaps unfortunate that the benefits were confined to those who channel their savings through an insurance company. The important consideration should have been to enable people to save for their retirement and whether the saving took the form of the accumulation of a capital sum or of the provision of a regular annual pension should have been immaterial so long as there were adequate safeguards against the use of the savings by the saver during the period of accumulation. Arrangements have been made for dealing with this in the Finance Act of 1969.

To meet the varying needs of taxpayers, insurance companies have made available a variety of policies. There are policies which are secured by fixed annual premiums and policies which are secured by single premiums, varying with the age attained. The former, which may be terminated and converted into fully paid policies, are more suitable for people in receipt of steady annual earned incomes. The latter, which may or may not be taken out as supplements to fixed annual premium policies, are more suitable for people with widely fluctuating annual incomes.

There are policies which provide for the return of premiums in the event of early death with interest or without interest, for pensions to run for a minimum of ten years or five years whether or not the pensioner survives, others to cease on the death of the pensioner; for pensions on the joint lives of a husband and wife; for pensions which aim to provide a safeguard against a possible future fall in the value of money; and for pensions with the additions of profits and without the addition of profits. In the case of "without profit" policies, the pensioner knows in advance exactly what he will receive as a pension on retirement; whereas in the case of "with profits" policies, he will know in advance only the basic pension which, as in the case of life assurances, will generally be lower than the pension obtainable under a "without profits" policy. In general there is little advantage in a "with profits" policy where the policy is taken out late in life. The assurer will also usually be wise to take out a pension guaranteed for a minimum number of years. The reduction in pension involved in a pension guaranteed for 5 years is negligible, for a man starting his pension at the age of 65. It is greater, of the order of 10% to 12%, where the guarantee is for 10 years.

Although subsequent tax changes have reduced, relative to other ways of providing for the future, some of the original attractions of these pensions, they still have advantages for those who are not covered or not covered adequately by an existing pension scheme, especially where they are supplemented by a temporary Life Assurance Policy to cover the early years of the pension policy, when the premium accumulations (and consequently the death benefit under the pension policy), remain small. Such supplementary Life Assurance Policies can be taken out at a surprisingly low cost.

National Savings

The term is misleading and is probably responsible for a good deal of confusion in the minds of the public. Sponsors of the various forms of national savings tend to leave in people's minds the idea that there is some special merit, for example in buying National Savings Certificates, not enjoyed by the acquisition of other types of investment. There is not, unless lending to the Government is more meritorious than lending to industry, which may indeed, on the contrary, put the money to a better use. Nor is there any special merit in the act of buying Savings Certificates. Any merit connected with such a purchase lies in the act of saving that may have preceded it. The mere purchase of National Savings Certificates out of the proceeds of the sale of other securities is negative from the national point of view and commendable from the investor's point of view, only if in the result he has improved the quality of his investment.

There are various forms of so-called national savings—the National Savings Certificates to which reference has been made and which were first introduced during the world war of 1914–18, Post Office and Trustee Savings Bank Deposits, 7% British Savings Bonds and Premium Savings Bonds. The chief advantage from the investor's point of view of each of these types of investment is that they may be realized at any time on short notice and without loss. In the case of National Savings Certificates there are limitations on the amount that may be invested in each issue (of which there have been 12); in the case of Post Office Savings Bank Deposits, limits on the amounts which may be deposited annually have been removed, but there is a limit of £5,000 on the total deposit which may be held. The special appeal of National Savings Certificates is that they are the only available form of wholly tax-free investment in this country. Not all issues however equally attractive. Those issued in earlier years bear rates of interest much lower than those borne by the 12th and latest issue, which was issued during a period of dear money.

The rate of interest obtainable on Post Office Savings Bank Deposits is 2½%, too low to attract the investor, even allowing for the fact that the first £15 of interest is free of income tax. Such Deposits are however unique in that within certain limits, they can be operated like an ordinary bank current account and yet unlike a bank current account they accumulate interest. They may also be operated at Post Offices throughout the country on presentation of the Deposit Book. Trustee Savings

TYPES OF PRIVATE INVESTMENT

Bank Deposits are akin to Post Office Savings Bank Deposits and differ mainly in the larger sums that may be withdrawn at any time.

7% British Savings Bonds are similar to other Government Securities and are distinctive only in that they may be realized without loss at any time on one month's notice. They are purchasable in amounts of £5 or multiples of £5 and are repayable at a premium of 2% on the first interest date, five years after purchase. Individual holdings are limited to £10,000.

Premium Savings Bonds are designed to attract the gambler. The holder, however, gambles not his capital but the income on his capital. The income that his capital would normally have earned is pooled and on the resulting pool lotteries are drawn. The holder of the lucky bond which represents an investment of only £1 may in the result win a maximum prize of £25,000 or other prizes ranging downwards from £1,000 to £25.

Tax Reserve Certificates are not classified as national savings although they fulfil the same functions. They may be purchased through banks in multiples of £5 and may be used for the settlement of income tax and surtax liabilities falling due within two years but not less than one month after their purchase. Provided that they are so used, interest accrues free of all tax, at rates which, depending upon the date of purchase, have varied in recent years between $2\frac{1}{4}$% and 4%.

Building Society Deposits and Shares and Bank Deposits

The legitimate functions of Building Societies are to provide funds for private house building. They lend money to house builders on the security of mortgages and borrow the money from depositors up and down the country and from people who are prepared to buy shares in the Society. Depositors lend the money subject to repayment on short notice. The rate of interest obtainable on such deposits is higher than that obtainable on Post Office and Trustee Savings Bank Deposits and is paid half-yearly free of income tax but not of surtax. On the other hand there is an extra risk arising from the fact that while the Societies borrow short they lend long. While people are prosperous and their savings are rising, no difficulty is likely to arise. When the reverse conditions apply, however, and people find it necessary to draw on their savings, Building Societies, owing to the long-term nature of their assets, might face serious difficulties in finding at short notice the money needed to repay their depositors. In such a situation, the only remedy might be a freezing of Deposits, thus cancelling one of their main virtues as investments, namely their liquidity. It is only fair to add in this connection that although Building Societies have existed for many years in this country and although they have lived through many different types of economic conditions, no freezing of Deposits has yet occurred.

The Shares of Building Societies offer a higher rate of return than their Deposits but ranking after them, they are much inferior in terms of the quality of security offered.

Bank Deposit accounts represent a convenient form of investment where the depositor has not yet decided on a permanent home for his money. The rates of interest obtainable on such deposits are generally low in relation to those obtainable on other forms of investment and are therefore attractive only while decisions of a more permanent character are being made.

Real Property

This may take the form of investment in land or in buildings. The buildings may be freehold, i.e. the ownership of the buildings may include the ownership of the land on which they are situated; or they may be leasehold, i.e. the ownership of the buildings may be separate from the ownership of the land on which they are situated. In the latter event the ownership of the buildings will eventually pass to the owner of the land, usually after 99 years from the beginning of the lease.

The kind of property in which the private investor is most likely to be interested is house property occupied by himself. This form of investment has everything to recommend it. It provides the owner, while he lives in it, with a guaranteed income, representing the rent which he would otherwise have to pay, free of tax and, if it is his main residence, of tax on any gain he may make on selling it, and with complete protection against the effects of inflation on the future cost of his housing. Buying a house with money borrowed from a Building Society, or Insurance company is for the same reasons one of the most useful forms of saving in which a young man can engage, full tax relief being available on the interest paid.

Property that he owns but is occupied by others falls into a different category. The most likely kind of property that he could own that would be used by others would be house property. Before acquiring it, he would be faced with the expense of having it surveyed and its value assessed in the light of prevailing property values. Then he would be faced with the legal expenses of having the property transferred to himself. Henceforth he would have the job of selecting tenants, fixing rents, collecting them, keeping the property in a proper state of repair and generally supervising his interest. The return he would receive would normally be a good one in relation to the capital sum he invested, but against this he would have worries greater than those which he would have had, had he decided on any other mode of investment. In a sense he would be in business, and if he had many properties in whole-time business, unless he has arranged to have the work of supervision transferred to agents working on his behalf.

Also, unlike any other investment he might have made, he may not be able to dispose of it easily. A prospective buyer will want to satisfy himself, as he earlier had satisfied himself, that it is a sound property to buy and that the price asked is a reasonable one. His rights of ownership are also liable to be interfered with by Government action. To protect tenants against rises in their rents resulting from war, Rent Restriction was introduced in the first war and extended in the second war. This had the effect of freezing rents and transferring to tenants the uninterrupted use of the properties occupied by them at the frozen rents. Steps have now been taken to remove some of the injustices of Rent Restriction but not until after severe losses have been incurred by landlords. The result has been the loss of a good deal of the value of certain classes of property as a method of investing against the risk of inflation.

In general, house property ownership, apart from ownership for one's own occupation, is not to be recommended as a form of investment, except for the expert who knows exactly what he is doing.

Property Mortgages and other Secured and Unsecured Private Loans

This is not a field into which the private investor should venture unless he has special knowledge of the property markets or wishes to back someone in business, or has other reasons of a personal character. Lending is a business and should be conducted as such. Private loans whether secured or unsecured may, depending on their terms, prove very renumerative investments but they are likely to remain personal and therefore difficult to terminate except with the consent of the borrower. Shakespeare's precept to the effect that one should "neither a borrower nor a lender be" applies very much to this field of investment. Where the borrower is not well versed in money matters, it is desirable in his own interests that the lender should be, except in those special cases where the claims of friendship appear to transcend those of ordinary business prudence. Then a gift might be more appropriate than a loan.

Marketable Securities

This is by far the widest field of investment open to the private investor and embraces almost every type of investment. The feature which distinguishes marketable securities from the types of investment which we have been considering is that while, like property, they have no settled price or realizable value, they may be realized at any time at a price determined by what buyers and sellers in a free market consider is reasonable. Governments or companies when they borrow money or raise capital, require the money over a long period of time, often perpetually. People who lend the money are usually unable or unwilling to lend the money for so long a period. The marketable security solves this difficulty, by assuring to the Government or the companies, as the case might be, the long-term finance they need and to the lender or subscriber, the means of realizing his investment at short notice. The buyer of a marketable security, whether it be a Government Loan or an industrial Ordinary share, undertakes however a risk, not undertaken for example by a Post Office Savings Bank depositor. The risk he undertakes is that he may not find anyone with the same faith in the Government Loan or the

TYPES OF PRIVATE INVESTMENT

Company Ordinary share, to pay him the price which he paid for it. He may receive a larger price or he may receive a smaller price but there is no guarantee that he will receive the same price.

Shareholders have often been criticized, because, having invested their money in a company, they do not remain permanently invested in that company. It is an unjust criticism. Shareholders do the job required of them when they subscribe for new capital. In that act, they provide the company irrevocably with the money it needs on the terms which the company demands. From then onwards the company has a responsibility to that shareholder and to any other shareholder who acquires his rights, for it was a condition of the original subscription that the rights could be transferred to a third party. Otherwise the subscription would not have been made.

Broadly speaking, Marketable Securities divide themselves into two main classes—Fixed Interest securities and Ordinary shares. To the former, which include Government Loans, Local Authority Loans and the Debentures, Loans and Preference stocks of companies, attach no special rights other than the rights to a fixed rate of interest or dividend and to repayment of the capital at a fixed price on the liquidation of the company or on redemption, if the securities are redeemable. To the latter attach the full rights and responsibilities of ownership subject to a limitation of the liability of their holders for the debts of the Company to the amount if any unpaid on the Shares; such "unpaid" liability is rare. Ordinary shares have normally no dividend rights other than the right to a dividend declared by the directors out of the profits of the company. Except where they are non-voting shares, they confer control of the company including the power to appoint the directors and dismiss them. In so far, however, as this control can only be enforced if the owners act collectively, it has in practice a limited value to individual owners.

When money is raised by a public issue of shares or stock, whether by a Government, a Local Authority or a Company, or by any other borrowing agency, a prospectus must be issued, giving a full description of the security to be issued. The description must include all known information which is likely to affect the quality of the security as an investment, such as the assets if any on which it will be secured, liabilities, the revenue or the sources of revenue from which interest payments will be made and the record of profits over a period of years, including the latest available profits, if the agency raising the money is a company. In the case of a new company which has not yet begun trading same indication of the future scope of the undertaking based on the opinion of experts must be given.

PART II MARKETABLE SECURITIES

CHAPTER III

THE RANGE AND MARKET OF MARKETABLE SECURITIES

The Range of Securities

With the exception of Life Assurance, which meets a specialized need, it is possible to find within the field of marketable securities most types of investment opportunities. There are, as we shall see, Government securities and Debenture stocks to meet the wishes of the investor who places security of income first in his scale of investment priorities. There are Government securities with early redemption dates to meet the needs of the investor who places security of capital first. And there are Ordinary shares and stocks of companies operating in most parts of the world and in almost every branch of activity, from which a selection can be made to satisfy the hopes of the investor whose main interest is to participate in the fruits of economic growth or whose main anxiety is the fear of inflation and the finding of ways and means of sheltering from its consequences.

Marketable securities embrace in fact an extremely wide field. The London Stock Exchange and Associated Stock Exchanges in the leading cities of this country handle every type of security, ranging from United Kingdom Government securities to the Debenture Preference and Ordinary stocks of every public company which has been formed in this country, or which has used the London market as its principal avenue for raising capital. Nor are the securities dealt in by members of the London Stock Exchange confined only to such securities. They extend to the securities of all countries which maintain Stock Exchanges. A London stockbroker can for example buy or sell the Common stocks (Ordinary stocks) of any American or Canadian company through connections he has established with American and Canadian brokers, at the very small additional cost of his own commission.

Normally, however, the main business of the London stockbroker will be with the buying and selling of securities officially dealt in on the London Stock Exchange. These securities, are detailed in a list which the London Stock Exchange publishes daily and are reproduced in the form of a monthly booklet by most of the leading firms of stockbrokers. This latter booklet which is issued free to clients, shows in addition to the prices of securities, their yields.

The list which is expensive to buy comprises some 10,000 securities ranging from United Kingdom Government securities at one end to highly speculative overseas mining and plantation companies at the other. The main sub-headings of the types of securities included in the list are shown in Appendix 1. Even these sub-headings do not however adequately describe the range of securities included. Under the heading Commercial and Industrial, for example, are concealed such important industries as general and electrical engineering, the motor, textile, food, tobacco, chemical and building industries as well as many others.

In addition to the name of each security, the list gives very approximately the price at which the security could be sold (the bid price) and the price at which it could be bought (the offered price) an hour before the close of business each day, together with the prices at which the security changed hands on that day or on the last day on which there were dealings. These last-mentioned prices, or markings as they are called, do not necessarily represent every transaction that has taken place in the shares, for there is no obligation on brokers or jobbers to record for publication every transaction they make. None the less such as they are and taken in conjunction with the approximate buying and selling prices of the security they give a reasonably good indication of the likely price of securities at the beginning of business on the following day. Extracts from the list relating to the prices of the more important securities are published daily in the Press.

The list is a comprehensive one and omits few forms of profit-making business. The counterpart of the village store is to be found in the chain or department store and the counterpart of the local builder in the many companies which are engaged in different branches of the building industry.

Counterparts are also to be found of the local shoemaker or repairer, the miller or the farmer. On the other hand the professions are seldom represented. Nor are certain industries represented which have in recent years been nationalized, such as railway transport, the coal industry, and the electric supply industry. The steel industry nationalized and then denationalized, has been brought again under public control. Sound broadcasting, the provision of postal services and telephones have for long been a field reserved to the Government and it is not therefore possible for the private investor to take an interest in them. On the other hand, television is already a highly profitable private enterprise; and it is possible for the investor to take an indirect interest in sound broadcasting and the telephone services through companies which manufacture equipment or, in the case of sound broadcasting, through companies which specialize in the relay of broadcasts.

Dealing in Marketable Securities

Prospective buyers and sellers of marketable securities may conduct their business either directly through a stockbroker or through a Unit Trust discussed elsewhere in this book or indirectly through their banks, their accountants or their solicitors where these undertake investment business. In either event the stockbroker is the key man whom the banks, the accountants and the solicitors must approach before any transaction can be put into effect. The stockbroker (hereinafter referred to as broker) must in turn make his way to a stockjobber or jobber, i.e. a specialist in the particular type of securities his client wishes to buy or sell. Jobbers on the London Stock Exchange are not allowed to have dealings with anybody who is not a member of the London Stock Exchange or his authorized clerk. Their function is to make a market in securities. They are ready at a price to buy any security or sell any security. Their profits unlike the profits of stockbrokers, which are dependent upon a fixed scale of commission, are dependent upon the difference between the price at which they are prepared to buy a share or stock and the price at which they are prepared to sell it. As they concentrate on a limited number of securities (there are jobbers who concentrate on Government securities, others on breweries and others on

South African gold mining shares, to take a few examples), and as there are many firms of jobbers in constant competition with one another, the prices they quote must be keen prices. The jobbers in all securities occupy one floor of the Stock Exchange, so that within a matter of seconds a broker with an order to execute can obtain quotations from three or four firms and have dealt with the jobber offering the best terms.

A broker receiving an order to buy or sell shares, will in fact approach several jobbers. Each will quote two prices and very probably different prices. One may quote 26s.–26s. 6d., another 26s. 1½d.–26s. 7½d. and another still, 25s. 10½d.–26s. 4½d. The broker will deal with the jobber who quotes the prices which most favours the interest of his client. The lower of the two prices which the jobber quotes represents what he is prepared to pay for the shares the broker, on behalf of his client, wishes to sell, and the higher of the two prices represents the price at which he is prepared to offer the shares the broker wishes to buy. The difference of 6d. per share represents the jobber's charge for the service of providing a market and of taking the risk that he might not be able to re-sell the shares if they are sold to him, or buy them back, if they are bought from him, on equally favourable terms. For jobbers will sell (bear) shares that they do not possess and buy (bull) shares for which they have no immediate buyer. In the one case they will eventually have to buy the shares back from someone else, perhaps at a higher price. In the other case, they may when they eventually find a buyer, have to sell the shares at a lower price than they paid for them.

The jobber's charge, or turn as it is called, will vary in accordance with whether the share is one which there is wide public interest or one in which the public interest is slight. If the share is one that is normally dealt in frequently because of a wide public interest, the jobber will have a reasonable expectation of selling without delay the shares that he has bought or of buying the shares he has sold, close to the price at which he has dealt. In that event he will feel able to quote a narrow price. Otherwise he will feel obliged to quote a wide price, to allow for the possibility that, when he comes to resell the shares if he has bought them, or buy them back if he has sold them, there may have been a change in the price of the shares, adverse to the way in which he wishes to deal.

Assuming that the investor when asking his broker to buy or sell shares for him has not limited his price, i.e. fixed a price below which he will not sell, or if he is a buyer, a price above which he will not buy, a deal will in the normal course of events take place. The broker will then make out a contract note which he will send to his client. This contract note will set out the number of shares bought or sold, the price at which the purchase or sale was made and the resulting cost or proceeds. To this cost will be added, or from the proceeds will be deducted the broker's commission plus a small nominal contract stamp. If the transaction was a purchase, there will be also added the cost of a 1% transfer stamp payable to the Government and a small registration fee usually of 2s. 6d. The 1% transfer stamp is with certain exceptions levied on the cost of the transfer of all registered securities, i.e. securities the title to which can only be transferred by a deed of transfer. The exceptions are United Kingdom, Commonwealth and Colonial Government securities and the securities of Local Authorities and certain other Public Bodies. Bearer securities, i.e. securities the title to which passes by hand, are subject on issue to a duty of 3% in the case of United Kingdom securities and to a duty of 2% in the case of overseas securities and are thereafter free of all duty on transfer.

Samples of a buying contract note and a selling contract note are given in Appendix II and the scale of broker's commissions in Appendix III.

The broker selling shares (or stock) will also send to his client a transfer form. This transfer form will state the seller's full name and address, the full description of the security sold, the number of shares or amount of stock sold and the consideration for the sale, i.e. the approximate proceeds. If the seller is satisfied that the particulars of sale as thus described are correct, he will sign the form and return it to his broker together with his share or stock certificate. This will complete the sale so far as he is concerned and unless he has purchased other shares or stock, he will be entitled to payment of the proceeds on the settlement date named in the contract note.

His broker will now send the form to the broker whose

client bought the shares. This latter broker will enter the full name, address and titles of the buyer on the form and send it to the company which issued the shares or stock, or to the Bank of England, if the security is a Government security, so that the transfer can be registered and a new certificate made out in the name of the buyer.

Whether the order is to buy shares or to sell shares, the investor is put to very little inconvenience. If he is a seller, he has to sign, unwitnessed, only once and despatch to his broker one set of documents; whereas if he is a buyer, having given the order to buy, there is no other action that he need take until called upon to pay. If he is both selling and buying, he need not receive or make out a cheque; his broker receives from the buyer and pays the seller for him. And from the expense point of view, it will make no difference whether he deals directly with a broker or indirectly through his bank. He will pay only one commission; in the latter case however the broker will share with his bank part of the commission he pays.

Income

Income paid on loans whether they are of Governments or Companies and whether they are secured, as in the case of Mortgages and Debentures, or unsecured, is usually termed interest. Income paid on companies' Preference shares (or stock), which are usually entitled to only a fixed rate of income, or on their Ordinary shares (or stock), on which the income is liable to fluctuate, is called dividend.

Interest and Preference dividends are usually paid at regular half-yearly intervals. In the case of Ordinary dividends practice varies. Some companies pay small interim dividends and large final dividends; others try to equalize as far as possible their interim and final dividends; and still others pay only final dividends, called in that case "annual", when they know what the results of the year have been as a whole. Ordinary dividends, being dependent each year on profits and on the decisions of the directors of companies taken in the light of these, are seldom paid precisely on the same day each year, as is the normal practice with interest payments and Preference dividends, but nevertheless are usually paid round about the same date.

With the exception of one or two Government stocks, for example 3½% War Loan, tax is deducted from all interest and dividend payments as they are made, at the standard rate of tax, i.e. for the present 8s. 3d. in the £, and therefore the investor normally receives his income net, as it is called. The object of this is to ensure that the Government collects from the investor the tax to which it is entitled. Where however the investor is not liable to pay tax, or is not liable to pay tax at the rate deducted, he may recover it from the Government.

Information

We have not so far described the information that is available regarding securities—information which in addition to the other work performed by brokers they must fully digest in order to give their clients an adequate service. Under the various Company Acts culminating in the Act of 1967, all public companies must publish the fullest information about their assets and liabilities and profits and dividends both in a Prospectus before making a public issue of their shares and at annual intervals thereafter. The accounts so published must give figures of turnover and of wage costs incurred in arriving at profits available to meet depreciation, directors' remuneration, taxation and if appropriate, Debenture interest and Preference dividends, and provide for reserves and dividends; they must also show total profits, including where appropriate the profits of all subsidiary companies, together with a Balance Sheet in which are stated all the assets of the company or group of companies as shown in their books, all the liabilities, including a statement of contingent liabilities, the Authorized and Issued Capital of the company and the reserves. With this information a record of profits can be made extending backwards many years, enabling the investor to form a very good judgment of the quality of the company in which he has invested or is contemplating making an investment.

Company accounts are however not the only source of information available to investors. Companies may be extremely well managed but conditions may be adverse to them. A company, for example, engaged in the production of copper is vitally dependent for its profits upon the demand for and price of copper. Reports on industries and on the prospects of industries are available and should therefore be studied if good judgments are to be formed. Such reports suffer, it is true, the same disadvantages as reports on company profits, in the sense that they relate to the past. None the less it is always possible, by a judicious sifting of information, to draw conclusions about the future of a company, which other less far-seeing investors may not be able to draw, and thus avoid losses from which others are unable to escape or make profits which others cannot acquire. Investment in marketable securities is not and is not intended to be risk-free investment. The risks (and of course the chances of profits which go with them) can however be reduced to the minimum or enlarged to the maximum in accordance with the aims of the investor, for there are securities to match every taste.

Summary

Marketable Securities cover a very wide range and provide instruments of investment suitable to every type of need. The value of capital invested in them is easy to appraise at any moment of time, since with very few exceptions there is always someone who will quote a price for them. By the same token they present no problems when valuations are needed for Estate Duty and other purposes. The Government is always ready to accept valuations based on the publicly quoted prices of securities. They are easy to deal in and the expenses of dealing are not high in relation to the advantages which may be obtained from a spread of good securities. There is an ample supply of information about them guaranteed by Governments through legislation for the protection of investors, although the Governments of some countries require less than others; and the existence of a free market is an assurance that at any moment of time the price of a stock whether it is to be bought or sold is a fair price in relation to all that is known about the stock at that time. Brokers are rewarded on a commission basis and are affected hardly at all by the prices at which purchases and sales of securities are effected; while the jobber when he quotes a price to a broker does not at the time know whether the broker intends to buy stock from him or sell stock to him. Should he therefore attempt to "read" the broker, by which is meant to guess whether he wants to buy or sell, and therefore to quote a price out of line with market conditions at the time, he might well find that he has bought stock from the broker at too high a price or sold stock to him at too low a price, i.e. in either case to his disadvantage and to the advantage of the broker's client.

CHAPTER IV

GENERAL INFLUENCES AFFECTING PRICES OF MARKETABLE SECURITIES

Yield

The worth of an investment is determined by the income it yields or is expected to yield. Let us take, for example, 2½% Consolidated Stock, the oldest existing Government security. This stock assures the holder a gross income of £2 10s. 0d. per annum in perpetuity on every nominal £100 of stock which he holds; but he can on no account claim his capital back from the Government. Now if 2½% is considered to be a reasonable rate of interest on a security of this type then the price of 2½% Consolidated Stock will be £100 for every nominal £100 of stock. The stock is then said to stand at par, which is another term for the face of nominal value. This was in fact the position shortly after the war when the Government was able to refund the original 3% Local Loans stock into the new 2½% Treasury stock (known colloquially as Daltons), thereby saving for the country ½% per annum on the stock refunded; but it is not the position now. In the meanwhile interest rates have risen, i.e. the yield which people consider a proper return on their money has risen. (What decides changes in interest rates is dealt with on pages 39 to 41.) Today people consider something like 5% a proper return on their money. They will only be ready to buy 2½% Consols at a price which will give them an income of £5 from every £100 cash invested. Since each £100 stock of Consols gives an income of only £2 10s. 0d. our investor will need to buy £200 stock with his £100 cash, if he is to get an income of £5 from that £100 cash. In other words he will only pay £50 cash for each £100 stock; the price is 50 and the yield is 5%.

Examples of how to calculate yield are given in Appendix IV, but these further explanations may be useful.

First, the price of the stock or share has to be adjusted for interest accrued. Between one interest (and in the case of a Preference stock dividend) payment and another interest is accumulating. During this period the stock is cum interest. A buyer of the stock will therefore be buying not only the capital stock but the amount of interest that has accumulated up to the date of his purchase. Likewise a seller of the stock will be selling, in addition to the stock, the amount of accumulated interest. When calculating the price that the buyer has paid for the stock, this interest should be deducted (and it should be deducted gross or net according to his tax position, i.e. according to whether he is liable to pay tax or not on the interest), for not only will he receive the capital stock but also interest which he has not earned. In the same way when calculating the price which a seller has received for the stock he has sold, interest should be deducted, since the accumulated interest is interest he has earned but will now have to go without.

Secondly, in due course and shortly before the interest (or dividend) is actually paid, the stock will be quoted ex interest (or dividend). Anybody buying thereafter will not receive the next interest payment; it will go to the seller. As the result the interest for the remainder of the period, at most a few weeks, will not be received by the buyer who has earned it and will be received by the seller who will not have earned it. In this case the price of the stock for purposes of yield calculation should be adjusted to allow for this by adding to the price the appropriate amount of interest, gross or net, still to accrue until the date of payment.

When dealing with Ordinary dividends, because they are not paid on fixed dates, if at all, and because an Ordinary dividend cannot be known for certain until it has been declared, the price is as a rule only adjusted when the dividend is declared and then only during the short period that elapses between the declaration of the dividend and the quotation of the Stock ex dividend. During that period the dividend is deducted from both the selling and the buying (i.e. the bid and offered) prices as in the case of Loan and Preference stocks cum interest or dividend payments.

Thirdly, price has to be adjusted for expenses; and in this respect a buyer approaches yield from a different point of view from that of a seller. A buyer is concerned with the yield he is going to receive on the total money he has to pay out including expenses, the seller with the yield on the net amount of money he will receive. Therefore in calculating yield for a buyer, expenses should be added to the price, whereas in calculating yield for a seller, expenses should be deducted.

Fourthly, interest and dividend payments on U.K. securities are usually expressed as a percentage of a nominal value of the stock or share. An investor may want to buy £100 (nominal) of Government stock or so many, say £1 (nominal) or 5s. (nominal), Ordinary shares. The interest or dividend he receives will be expressed as a percentage related to these figures and not to the price he pays. For example, a 4% Government stock will give an income of £4 per £100 of stock and a £1 Ordinary share, paying a dividend of 25%, an income of 5s. or £¼. If the price of the one is 80 and of the other £5 the yield will in each case be 5%, i.e. 4 × 100 ÷ 80 = 5; and ¼ × 100 ÷ 5 = 5.

The Rate of Interest

The prices of all securities are affected in greater or lesser degree by changes in the rate of interest. Securities where there is an obligation on the part of the Government or other borrower to repay the principal sum borrowed at an early date—say in a year—are, however, very largely insulated from the effects of such changes. In their case, the fall in price resulting from a rise in expected rates of interest, will be checked by the knowledge that within a year at the latest the Government will be obliged to repay £100 cash for every £100 nominal of the stock. If for example the stock is a 2½% stock issued at a time when interests rates were very low, a buyer of the stock will be assured of an all-in income of at least £5 for every £100 he invests, if he pays a price for the stock somewhere between 97½ and 98. If he pays 97½ he will be able to buy approximately £102 10s. 0d. of stock. On this he will receive an income of slightly more than £2 10s. 0d. and at the end of the year or earlier he will receive £102 10s. 0d. from the Government in repayment of his holding. In all he will therefore receive rather more than £105 in return for the original £100 he invested.

The foregoing illustration and the illustration on page 36, serve to show that the expectation of income received one way

GENERAL INFLUENCES AFFECTING PRICES 39

or another from a stock settles what has to be valued, and that the prevailing rate of interest settles how it is to be valued. Where a stock is a perpetual stock, i.e. a stock where the borrower or issuer has no obligation to repay the principal sum but must make regular annual interest payments in perpetuity, the rate of interest exerts its maximum influence in determining the price of the stock. Where on the other hand the borrower or issuer has an obligation to repay the principal sometime in the future, the rate of interest exerts less influence on the price the nearer the stock is in point of time to its date of redemption.

The reliability of the income from each security and each class of security will be variously esteemed. If the income from the security is thought to be unreliable the immediate rate of yield appropriate to that security will be high. The converse will also be true; but in both cases the rate of yield will be affected by the prevailing general rate of interest applying to all securities.

How the Rate of Interest is decided

What decides the general rate of interest? We saw in Chapter 1 how important it is from the general economic standpoint that new saving and new investment should proceed in step with one another in such a way that the states identified as inflation, i.e. rising prices and a falling value of money, and deflation, i.e. falling profits and diminishing employment, should both be avoided. The one state we saw is the outcome of the demands for money to finance new investment outrunning the supply of savings at the existing level of prices. The other state is the outcome of the supply of savings at the existing level of economic activity outrunning the demands for money to finance new investment. Both states are undesirable and it is the aim of modern Governments to restore an equilibrium, in the one case by checking new investment demands and in the other by encouraging them.

The quickest acting instrument for achieving this is the Government's control over the supply and cost of money. How this control operates is explained in more detail in Appendix V but in brief what it amounts to is that the Government arbitrarily raises or lowers the rate of interest. It does this in the first place by changing the Bank Rate, the rate of interest charged by the Bank of England to its customers for temporary accommodation or for discounting bills. This action it reinforces by reducing or, as the case might be, increasing the ability of the other Banks to lend money.

The clearing banks are guided in their lending operations by the amount of cash they hold in their tills and on deposit with the Bank of England and to a lesser extent by the amount of their liquid assets. The Bank of England can reduce or increase the amount of cash by selling or buying securities in the market. The Clearing Banks in the result having less money or more money to lend have an immediate incentive to follow the Bank of England's lead by raising or lowering their own lending rates. At this stage the entire community becomes involved. New investors have to pay a higher rate or a lower rate of interest for the money they want to borrow. They may even find it impossible to raise the money they need. In any event whether they manage to raise it or not they will be confronted with a totally changed investment climate. If the rate of interest has been raised, the profits they had hoped to make from the exploration, say, of some new invention will look thinner and they will no longer have quite the same assurance of an expanding market for the products of their investment when it has been completed. If on the other hand the rate of interest has been lowered, not only will they find it easier and cheaper to borrow against new projects but they will experience a general sense of relief that action is being taken to deal with the falling level of profits and diminishing employment that was threatening. Security prices will tend to rise owing to the effects of the lower level of interest rates and altogether a greater sense of economic well-being will replace the growing sense of despondency that preceded it.

In order to curb inflation, or as the case may be deflation, the Government is not however obliged, in the longer run, to rely on action through the rate of interest. Through the Budget it has the power to transform an inflationary situation into a deflationary one and a deflationary one into an inflationary one. It can for example reduce the general level of demand, if it is inflation it wants to correct, by reducing its own expenditures, or by increasing taxes, thus leaving the public with

GENERAL INFLUENCES AFFECTING PRICES 41

less of its income to spend; or it can increase the level of demand, if it is deflation it wants to correct, by increasing its own expenditures or by reducing the taxes the public has to pay, thereby leaving it with a larger income to spend. It is as well to keep this in mind, by not assuming too automatically that the existence of inflation implies a permanently higher level of interest rates and the converse. Government policy has much more to do with the rate of interest than is generally supposed.

The Balance of Payments

Nations must trade with one another—some more than others. The United Kingdom is one of the large traders. It is also the financial centre of a Commonwealth. These reasons require the United Kingdom pound (sterling) to be a currency in which foreigners have confidence. Foreigners will have little confidence in a currency which is being continually inflated and so losing value.

In order to meet our payments in foreign currencies as they fall due, for goods and services imported, the Government keeps a reserve of Foreign Exchange. This reserve is held in the form of gold and dollars which are freely exchangeable into other currencies. When we are suffering from inflation we get into difficulties with our foreign payments. High internal demands—a profitable home market—discourage exports. They also drive up imports. We begin to buy more from abroad than we sell abroad. In the end, in order to pay our way, we have to use up gold and dollar reserves. Knowing that these are small the Government gets worried and is forced to cut down internal demands. Its way of doing this is to raise interest rates. In fact Balance of Payments difficulties are merely one facet of the general problem of inflation.

But as with inflation so with the Balance of Payments, action on the rate of interest is not the only alternative although it has been the one most favoured by post-war Conservative Administrations. Another alternative is the application of tighter exchange control, by the adoption or re-adoption of import licensing. The weakness of this approach is that it tackles only the symptoms and, unless supplemented by other action to control internal demands, the effect would be to transfer the main impact of inflation from the Balance of Payments to the home market, creating shortages of goods and necessitating other controls.

There is yet another alternative—the lowering of the exchange value of the pound. This alternative has been tried twice by a Labour Government in recent times with most unhappy results. Devaluation of a currency undermines confidence in money itself and is apt for that reason to promote the "flight" out of money which it is one of its aims to check. For a time it lowers the prices of the country's goods to foreigners, making foreigners want to buy more from us and raises the prices of imported goods, making home consumers want to buy less foreign goods. If, however, simultaneously with devaluation home demand is kept artificially high, extra goods do not become available for export and the demand for imported goods remains higher than it should be. Yet if problems of internal inflation are persistently neglected, a devaluation of sterling cannot be permanently avoided either by Governments of the Right or of the Left. Both are involved in the fact that a steady rise in the prices of British goods unmatched by similar rises in the prices of goods manufactured in other countries will result in excessive imports and diminished exports and in the long run in an inability to make ends meet without a lowering of the price of sterling in terms of the prices of other currencies.

The Balance of Payments may therefore react on the rate of interest but it may also react on the price of sterling. If it reacts on the price of sterling it will have investment consequences almost as far reaching. It will raise the sterling price of gold and it will raise the prices to a British holder of the securities of all countries which have not been forced by the same circumstances to devalue their currencies. It will favour the exporting industries and curb the importing industries.

General Economic Conditions

Where the income from a security depends upon profits, the price of the security will be vitally affected by the profits of the company and particularly by the prospects of future profits. These profits will depend partly on the skill of the management but also partly on the general conditions of trade affecting the industry in which the company operates. These conditions will in turn depend on the state of the economy, on the skill with which the Government is managing it and on economic conditions in the world generally. As already noted, the United Kingdom is one of the large world traders and many of its leading industries are heavily dependent for their prosperity on what they are able to sell to customers overseas. If for any reason overseas customers lose their buying power the consequences for these industries will be serious. Nor will the consequences be confined to these industries. As they are important customers of other industries, the effects will spread, making it very difficult for the Government with the best intentions to maintain the overall level of economic activity and employment. Profits generally will suffer, dividends will decline and investors will cease to value Ordinary shares, as a class, as highly as they previously did.

The investor must therefore in his own interest watch the general economic situation and also, if he can, economic conditions in the world at large and especially in the United States. The United States consumes a very substantial proportion of the industrial raw materials produced by the world outside Russia. If therefore anything happens to disturb economic conditions in the United States there are repercussions in all the other markets of the world, through the influence on prices of changes in American buying. If the United States becomes a much reduced buyer of commodities world commodity prices fall. Lower commodity prices mean a fall in the purchasing power of the raw material producing countries to which the United Kingdom sells a large proportion of its manufactured goods. A fall in world commodity prices having its origins in the collapse of the American economy in 1929 began the last great world economic depression. It could mark the beginning of another world economic depression but for one important difference—the responsibilities which Governments have assumed not only in the United Kingdom but also in the United States for seeing that the overall level of domestic demand is held at levels sufficient to keep their people and their industries in reasonably full employment.

Inflation

Arising out of these responsibilities a new problem or at least a new problem for the British investor has arisen—that of deciding whether inflation has become a permanent feature of capitalism in its new development. We argued earlier that Governments are determined to fight it but we also argued that Governments are equally if not more determined to fight its opposite—deflation and unemployment. Wage and price increases, once they occur, are difficult to eliminate without repercussions on employment and output and without the threat of industrial strife which as yet Governments have shown a reluctance to face. If output and employment threaten to decline Governments are at once placed under strong pressure to reverse the actions which brought about the decline or to take actions which reverse the decline. Not for many years has any Government spokesman suggested that wages might be reduced. The maintenance of a high overall level of economic activity, as it has so far operated, has therefore been a one-way operation so far as prices and what money will buy (the value of money) is concerned. Wages and prices have risen. When the pace has been too rapid it has been checked (but not reversed) until the worst effects, chiefly those on the balance of payments, have been removed. Then, when employment waned, inflation has been resumed leading to a still higher level of wages and prices. That at least has been the experience of the United Kingdom. Success in combating inflation and yet maintaining a high overall level of economic activity has been greater in the United States, although even in that country it cannot be said with confidence that the battle has yet been won.

In these circumstances it is natural for investors to search for every means of preserving the value of their savings. Fixed Interest securities expose them to the full effects of inflation because the income from them is fixed in terms of money and the value of the income as prices rise is constantly diminishing. Ordinary shares on the other hand provide them with some chance of protection. Under conditions of inflation profits rise. As profits rise dividends rise and although shareholders may in the long run be no better off with their increased dividends than they would have been if dividends

GENERAL INFLUENCES AFFECTING PRICES 45

had not been increased and there had been no inflation, they may not be worse off, as they certainly will be if in the same circumstances they hold nothing but Fixed Interest securities, even of the very highest quality. Investors will begin to sell their Fixed Interest securities and buy Ordinary shares, lowering the prices of the former reatively to the latter.

Politics

Political influences on Security markets are many and various, ranging from the constructive measures taken by Governments to maintain the Nation's economic health—measures against inflation and measures against depression—to the destructive measures aimed at depriving investors of some of their rights. In general investors favour Conservative administrations and distrust Socialist administrations, and for reasons which are easy to understand. Socialists are opposed to Capitalism. They are prepared to work with it in the knowledge that they cannot achieve full Socialism at once but their constant aim is to limit the power and the privileges of the individual Capitalist, and to bring within the field of Government control, a larger and ever larger share of the Country's economic activities.

To suggest that all Socialist measures are destructive, and all Conservative measures are constructive from the investor's point of view would, however, be going too far. Post-war Conservative administrations have not succeeded in dealing with the problem of inflation. They have as the result delivered heavy punishment to the investors in all Fixed Interest securities including U.K. Government securities. They have made extensive use of interest rate policy to combat inflation and no use of the Budget. While this has brought temporary advantages to the new saver in the form of a higher rate of interest, it has brought serious disadvantages to the old investor in Fixed Interest securities, who has suffered, as a consequence, sharp falls in the capital values of his investments, in addition to the falls in their real values. Labour administrations have not shown themselves to be any more adept at looking after the interests of the Fixed Interest investor. Instead of fashioning new instruments of control appropriate to the socialist goals they were hoping to reach, they adopted too readily the methods of their predecessors, in the vain belief that somehow they could manage things better. They could not. They could do things differently, with a different social objective in view, but they could not do things as well with substantially the same social objective in view. The contribution they could have made and should have made was to bring monetary management up-to-date with the needs of an economy determined to avoid another slump, yet able to live within its means without the recurrent dislocating effects of goods shortages and undue price rises, damaging to enterprising business and sound economic growth. This contribution they may yet make but the time is already late. Their chief success from the investor's point of view to date has been a remarkable boom in Ordinary share prices based alas less on belief in the future of economic growth than on fear for the future of the pound.

Political considerations are not confined to the home front. They apply all over the world—racial problems in South Africa—left-wing nationalism in the Middle East where this country gets most of its oil and owns much of it—and chronic political instability in the South American Republics. There is in fact enough trouble elsewhere to induce the belief that there is much to be said for investment at home, where the risks being our own are easier to assess and where the opportunities are considerable, if the investor knows what to do.

CHAPTER V

FIXED INTEREST SECURITIES—
GENERAL

Description

Fixed Interest securities are so described because they entitle the holder to a fixed annual payment of interest or dividend so long as the securities remain outstanding, i.e. until they are repaid by the original borrower or issuer. The terms of the securities may provide for repayment at a particular time, in which event they will be called redeemable or dated securities or they may make no such provision, in which event they will be called perpetual, irredeemable or undated securities. There are as might be expected many kinds of Fixed Interest securities. The commonest are those issued by Governments. Governments when they borrow usually raise the money they require in the form of loans with a fixed rate of interest payable half yearly, and redeemable after a specified number of years at par, that is to say, £100 per £100 of nominal stock issued. The stock may be issued at par but this is the exception rather than the rule. The chief reason is that Governments, and for that matter other borrowers, like their loans to conform to certain conventional rates such as 3%, $3\frac{1}{2}\%$, 4% or even $4\frac{1}{4}\%$ but very seldom if ever $4\frac{1}{8}\%$, and that the existing pattern of interest rates is very unlikely to coincide exactly with any one of these rates at the precise time the Government wants to raise new money. To give a simple example, suppose that the prevailing rate of interest for a Government security with no fixed date of redemption is $4\frac{1}{3}\%$ and suppose that the Government wants to raise some new money and that it wants to raise the money without committing itself to any final date of redemption. If the new issue is to have the best chance of success the Government will have to offer a yield of say $4\frac{3}{8}\%$, which is just a little over $4\frac{1}{3}\%$. But as has already been explained $4\frac{3}{8}\%$ is an unusual rate of interest for the Government to adopt. It will therefore probably decide to issue a $4\frac{1}{4}\%$ or a 4% stock.

There will be no possibility however of investors paying £100 for £100 of 4% stock. They will want a yield of at least $4\frac{3}{8}\%$. So the Government will issue the stock at $\dfrac{100 \times 4}{4\frac{3}{8}}$ or £91·43, say £91¼ per £100 nominal of stock. That is to say the Government will issue a 4% stock entitling the subscriber to £4 of interest for every £100 of stock subscribed at £91¼. The stock will give a yield to the subscriber of $\dfrac{£4 \times 100}{91\frac{1}{4}}\% = £4$ 7s. 8d. compared with the current yield available on a similar stock of £4 6s. 8d.

The principles underlying the issue of redeemable securities are the same as those underlying the issue of securities without fixed redemption dates. That is to say the Government will have to make the price attractive and the loan will carry a rate of interest which does not exactly coincide with the current market rate for such securities.

The Government in deciding what kind of loan to issue will take account of what kind of loan the investing public is most likely to want. For example, institutions and especially insurance companies with life policies likely to mature over a period of years, like their investments where possible to fit in with these expected maturities. The Government, providing as it does a very large proportion of the marketable investments available to the public, has the opportunity of meeting these needs by arranging that at intervals of every year or two, one or other of its loans will fall due for redemption. In this way the Government can meet the demand and therefore secure for itself the best available borrowing terms.

In arranging its redemption dates in this way the Government and for that matter any other type of borrower likes to avoid having to redeem a stock on a specific day. Conditions on that day or round about that day may be unsuitable for the raising of money. The Government and other borrowers much prefer to have a year or two years in which to choose the precise redemption dates for their loans. At one time they demanded much longer periods. As an example the original 5% War Loan was redeemable at any time between 1929 and 1947. (It was in fact redeemed in 1932 when it was

FIXED INTEREST SECURITIES—GENERAL

replaced by the present 3½% issue.) Modern practice does not however favour such long periods of redemption and stocks with as wide a gap between their first and last dates of redemption are generally unpopular with the investing public. Popular maturity or redemption periods are now confined to two or three years and there are a number of Government stocks, for example 5¼% Conversion Loan 1974, which have only one redemption date.

Where a stock has a first and a last date of redemption, it is assumed that the borrower, i.e. the Government, will redeem the stock on the first date, if in doing so it can raise money on cheaper terms and on the last date if the contrary is the case. That is to say a stock standing above par, because the current rate of interest is lower than the rate of interest which the stock bears, is assumed to be redeemable on the first date, and a stock standing below par, because the current rate of interest is higher than the rate of interest which the stock bears, is assumed to be redeemable on the last date.

Yields on Redeemable Securities

Because of the obligations of the borrower, in this case the Government, to repay its loan by a certain time, whatever the circumstances at that time may be, the prices of redeemable securities are as we noted in the previous chapter, less affected by changes in the rate of interest. If the rate of interest which an investor expects on a Government security is 5%, an irredeemable security which pays only 3½% per £100 nominal of stock will be worth not £100 but £70, for only at a price of £70 per £100 of stock will he be able to secure the 5% yield he considers necessary. But if the security is a redeemable one, say finally in 10 years, whatever happens to the price of the security between now and then, there is a certainty that it will be worth £100 per £100 of stock in 10 years.

The security will not be worth £100 now because at £100 the investor will be able to earn only 3½% on his money. The price will have to be less than this. Suppose for the sake of example the price is £85 and that the investor pays this for it. At a price of £85 he will be getting a yield of slightly more than 4% on the £3 10s. 0d. which the security pays annually $\left(\dfrac{£3 \text{ 10s. 0d.} \times 100}{85} = £4\cdot1\%\right)$, compared with the 5% he would have received on a non-redeemable security. In addition however he will be guaranteed a capital profit of £15 (the difference between £85 and £100) when the security is redeemed in 10 years. This capital profit unlike the interest he receives annually will be tax free in the case of a Government security, where the gain is exempt from capital gains tax, but not in the case of other Fixed Interest securities, where the gain is subject to tax. (See page 142.) If he is a taxpayer it will therefore be worth more to him than it would be if he received it as income. On the other hand he will not receive it until after 10 years have elapsed which will mean that its value will not be so much to him as it would have been if he had received it, as he receives his interest, in annual instalments.

Taking these two considerations into account, the tax free element in the capital profit and the fact that the profit cannot be realized until after 10 years have elapsed, the capital profit might be worth the equivalent of 2% per annum subject to tax on the price he pays for the stock. In that event the equivalent yield to him on his whole investment if he buys the security at £85 will be over 6%, which is more than 1% better than the yield on a $3\frac{1}{2}$% irredeemable stock standing 15 points lower at £70. In the circumstances the price of the $3\frac{1}{2}$% redeemable stock is likely to be more than £85.

The comparison of the yields on redeemable and on irredeemable securities is in fact not a straightforward matter. Yet investors will require a much more precise assessment of yields than that which has just been offered if they are to make up their minds which is the cheaper, the $3\frac{1}{2}$% irredeemable stock standing at £70 or the $3\frac{1}{2}$% 10-year redeemable stock standing at £85. This is done for them by experts using actuarial tables. The yields (for an explanation see Appendix VI) on redeemable stocks are calculated on three bases—

The Current Yield is calculated on the same basis as the yield on irredeemable securities, i.e. by dividing the income from the security by the price and multiplying the result by 100.

The Gross Redemption Yield is the current yield added to

FIXED INTEREST SECURITIES—GENERAL

the capital profit on redemption or less the capital loss if the stock is standing above par adjusted where appropriate for capital gains tax, the profit or loss being expressed as so much per cent per annum on the price of the stock.

The Net Redemption Yield is the current yield less income tax added to the capital profit on redemption, or less the capital loss if the stock is standing above par again adjusted where appropriate for capital gains tax, the profit or loss being expressed again as so much per cent per annum on the price of the stock.

If the investor is exempt from income and capital gains tax because his income is low or for other reasons, it will be the gross redemption yield that will concern him and it will be this that he will want to compare with the yields available on other securities. If on the other hand he is a taxpayer, it is the net redemption yield which will concern him and which he will want to compare with the net yields available on other securities.

The following example illustrates the various types of yields and how those on one redeemable stock compare with one which has no fixed date of redemption.

Name of Stock	Price 16/5/69	Current Yields Gross %	Net %	Redemption Gross %	Yields Net %
3½% War Loan	38¼d	9 1 0	5 6 4	— — —	— — —
3½% Electricity 1976–79	64⅝d	5 8 6	3 3 9	8 14 6	6 9 9

In terms of current yields 3½% War Loan is much the cheaper stock but unless there is a fall in interest rates over the following 10 years redemption yields favour 3½% Electricity Stock after allowance for tax.

Redeemable and Irredeemable Securities Compared

Redeemable Securities alone guarantee the payment of a specified capital sum by a certain date. As a result there is a certainty that whatever their prices may be now they will stand at their redemption prices, usually par, by the time they are redeemed. For this reason, unless there is a change in the general level of interest rates, they will rise in price the nearer they approach their redemption dates. Equally, the nearer they approach their redemption dates the less their prices will be affected by changes in interest rates. Securities with early redemption dates are therefore the safest from the capital point of view.

Just because redeemable securities are the safest type of Fixed Interest security from the capital point of view, it does not necessarily follow that under all circumstances they will be the most successful from the investment point of view. All depends on what the future level of interest rates is likely to be. If the future level of interest rates should be higher than the current level, then the advantage will prove to have lain with the redeemable stock. The prices of irredeemable stocks will suffer a fall which will fully reflect the rise in interest rates, but the price of the redeemable stock will be protected by the anchor provided by the certainty that the stock will in due course be redeemed at an agreed price. Moreover on re-investment, income will be increased on account of the rise in interest rates. If on the other hand the future level of interest rates should be lower than the current level, opposite considerations will apply. The anchor provided by the redeemable stock will act as a drag while the price of the stock without a fixed redemption date standing well below par will rise to reflect fully the drop in interest rates. $2\frac{1}{2}\%$ Treasury Stock, which has no fixed date of redemption, standing at £53 per £100 of stock on 17 February 1959, offered a yield of $4\frac{3}{4}\%$. If the yield were to fall to $3\frac{1}{2}\%$, the price of the stock would rise to £$71\frac{1}{2}$ or by 35%. On the same day $2\frac{1}{2}\%$ Savings Bonds 1964–67 standing at £86 offered a gross redemption yield of just under $4\frac{3}{4}\%$. If the gross redemption yield were to fall also to $3\frac{1}{2}\%$ the price would rise to £$93\frac{3}{4}$ or by only 9·0%.

Accordingly in selecting securities and in deciding between securities with fixed dates of redemption and securities without, investors will first want to ask themselves what the future level of interest rates is likely to be in relation to present rates. Having formed a view (and having formed the view, let us say, that they are likely to fall) they will then want to buy securities which safeguard their existing income for the longest period ahead. The securities which will best achieve this will be those without fixed redemption dates which stand well below par and which are therefore unlikely to be redeemed unless there is a very sharp fall in interest rates, or those which may not in any event be redeemed until very many years have elapsed. When interest rates are high the former, if they are low-couponed stocks (that is to say stocks carrying a low nominal rate of interest such as $2\frac{1}{2}\%$ Treasury Stock) standing well below par, may offer the best protection of income, whereas when interest rates are already low and most securities are standing close to or above par, the advantages will lie with securities with the longest periods to run before their first redemption dates are reached.

When investors anticipate a future rise in interest rates, converse considerations will apply. They will then be less concerned with the perpetuation of their income, which they will hope to increase. They will therefore prefer securities with early final dates of redemption, the proceeds of which, when they are repaid, will be able to earn the higher rates of interest expected.

The Quality of Securities

Fixed Interest securities vary greatly in quality and the yields which they offer vary accordingly. With Fixed Interest securities, the credit-worthiness of the borrower in the case of a Loan and the adequacy and security of the profits out of which the dividend is paid, in the case of a Preference Stock, are the most important considerations in determining their values. For the essence of Fixed Interest securities is that their interest should not vary from year to year but should remain constant in terms of money. Yields are therefore lowest, i.e. prices are highest in relation to income, on those securities which appear to offer the safest income in the future and highest on those which appear to offer the least safe income in the future. This variation of yield may or may not compensate the holder of high yielding Fixed Interest securities for the extra risks he incurs in holding them, but it does justify him in preferring as investments the high yielding to the low yielding ones where he believes the risks attaching to the former to be exaggerated or the risks attaching to the latter to be underestimated.

Where interest payments are suspended or Preference dividends are "passed" (the technical term for failure to pay

Preference dividends at their due date), the Fixed Interest security in question will cease to provide any income and therefore yield. It will not for that reason cease to have any value. The value will then depend on the likelihood of regular interest or dividend payments being ultimately resumed and on the value of any arrears of interest or dividend (if the Preference stock is a cumulative Preference stock) that may have accumulated in the meanwhile. Where the reason for the suspension is the declared inability of some foreign Government to meet its overseas commitments investors will generally take a pessimistic view of future prospects, for when this happens the cause has generally less to do with the foreign Government's inability to meet its commitments than with its reluctance to put its economy in a state where these commitments can be met. A degree of dishonesty will in other words be suspected which will be expected to persist. Where on the other hand the reason for the suspension is loss of earning power on the part of a company or other borrowing institution, investors will value their future expectations in much the same way as they would value their future expectations from an Ordinary share, that is to say by reference to the chances of a future recovery of the lost earning power.

Apart from the quality of individual Fixed Interest securities, the quality of Fixed Interest securities in general is greatly affected by what happens in the future to the value of money. Entitling holders to fixed annual payments in money, they make no provision for the possibility that money in the future may have a lower purchasing value than it has today. Equally they will confer benefits on holders should the purchasing value of money increase in the future. In the light of the economic history of the past twenty years and of contemporary tendencies, the prospect of the latter seems, however, small compared with the risk of the former.

CHAPTER VI

CLASSES OF FIXED INTEREST SECURITIES

The Range

The main classes of Fixed Interest securities are United Kingdom Government Loans, the Loans of our Local Authorities (counties and cities) and Public Authorities (Docks, Harbours and Water Boards) and the Loans Debentures and Preference stocks of privately operated public companies registered in the United Kingdom. There are in addition a special group of Water stocks as well as a wide selection of Foreign and Commonwealth Government, Local Authority and company Debenture and Preference stocks. We shall direct our attention here mainly to Sterling securities as, although the principles applying to foreign and other overseas stocks are substantially the same, owing to differences of political and economic circumstances, risks can be very different. For example a German or a Japanese Government loan, payable in the currencies of these countries, can never be to a British holder the straightforward security that one of the loans of his own Government is to him. There is first the fact that we have in the past been at war with these countries and could conceivably again be at war with them. There is no certainty therefore that in spite of the credit-worthiness of the two Governments, interest payments will be regularly met and that the obligations to redeem, if they carry such obligations, will be met at their due dates. There is also the economic difficulty that whereas a foreign Government may usually be relied upon to find in its own currency the money needed to pay the obligations on its loans, it may at any time run into Balance of Payments difficulties which may make it difficult for it to convert the interest or capital payments into Sterling. This has often happened with foreign loans—with South American loans, with European loans and with Far Eastern loans and has led to defaults, in consequence of which the British investor has lost much of the capital which he had originally invested.

In the past the pound Sterling was a strong currency; relative to which many currencies were weak. As a result prejudices developed against foreign loans as a medium of investment. In recent years however the position of Sterling has changed. In consequence some foreign loans may today be looked upon, not so much as another type of Fixed Interest security but as a means of hedging against the risk of a future fall in the value of Sterling.

British Government Securities

The Government's total Debt internal and external on 31 March 1958 was approximately £27,000 million. Of this total approximately £3,800 million was Funded Debt, i.e. Debt which the Government has no obligation ultimately to redeem and £21,400 million Internal Unfunded Debt, i.e. Internal Debt which the Government must sooner or later redeem. The rest of the Debt was either External Debt, or Debt to International Institutions such as the International Monetary Fund.

All of the Funded Debt, with the exception of small Debts to the Banks of England and Ireland, is publicly quoted and consists of such well-known securities as 2½% Consols, 3½% Conversion Loan and 3½% War Loan. The bulk of the Internal Unfunded Debt is either publicly quoted or consists of easily realizable securities such as National Savings Certificates, Defence Bonds, Tax Reserve Certificates and Treasury Bills.

The British Government as a borrower has a higher credit rating than any other class of British borrower. Because the Government is also much the largest borrower, its loans are more widely held than the loans of any other organization or institution in this country. The result is that they are very much easier to buy and to sell than any other class of security. It is possible for example at most times to buy or sell £1,000,000 of Government stock without changing the price more than ⅛% or ¼% and sometimes without changing the price at all. This could happen with no other security. To buy or sell £1,000,000 stock of any other group, organization or authority would involve buying or selling a large proportion of the total issue outstanding, whereas to buy or to sell a similar amount of Government stock would involve only a small proportion of the total issue outstanding.

There are Government securities to meet the needs of the investor who attaches most importance to the safeguarding of his capital. There are also Government securities to meet the needs of the investor who wants a secure money income over the longest possible period. If the investor attaches great importance to the security of his capital there is an ample supply of short-dated Government securities, including Treasury Bills, from which he can make his selection. If he is prepared to run a greater risk with his capital in the meanwhile without risking it in the long run, he can guarantee his income for a longer period by buying one of the many medium-dated securities, i.e. securities which are finally redeemable in 10 to 20 years; while if he wishes to look even further ahead, there is one security with a guaranteed life of nearly 40 years and several securities with lives which must be perpetual unless interest rates fall to something like half their present level, when it would become worthwhile and possible for the Government to redeem them with the proceeds of an issue bearing a lower rate of interest. Meanwhile of course these securities would have doubled or nearly doubled in price. One such security is $2\frac{1}{2}\%$ Consols. $2\frac{1}{2}\%$ Treasury Stock falls into the same category but enjoys the additional advantage of not being redeemable until after 1 April 1975.

The main characteristics of Government securities are then, their high quality, the ease with which they can be bought and sold and their variety. Additional advantages are, the exemption of gains on disposal from capital gains tax and that in common with Commonwealth, Local Authority and certain Public Board stocks, which are discussed later, no stamp duty is payable on their transfer. On the other hand and as would be expected, they offer lower yields than other classes of Fixed Interest securities.

Commonwealth and Colonial Government Securities

A wide selection of these securities is available on the London market. The principal Commonwealth securities are the Sterling loans of the Australian and New Zealand Governments. Their investment status in the eyes of British investors is slightly lower than that of British Government securities. They offer therefore higher yields but not so much higher as to justify the investor exchanging his British Government holdings for them. There are extra risks to British holders in the loans, for they require the Australian and New Zealand Governments to find not merely enough of their own currency in order to pay interest on them but enough Sterling also into which to convert the interest. No doubt these Governments will always be able to meet their commitments but there have been times in the past when there were serious doubts about their ability to do so.

The investment status of the Sterling loans of most of the other Commonwealth and Colonial Governments has changed greatly in recent years. South Africa has ceased to be a member of the Commonwealth while many of the former Colonies have become self-governing. Being new to the responsibilities of government a good deal of doubt naturally exists as to how these new countries will measure up to them in the long run. The yields on the loans which they have taken over from their predecessors have as the result risen considerably. Only time will tell whether this discounting of future risks has been over-done. Meanwhile the ordinary investor will be well advised to leave investment in the loans to others better equipped than himself to appraise the risks.

Local Authority Stocks

These consist of the loans of the principal counties, cities and towns of Great Britain and Northern Ireland and are similar in type to Government securities. They are secured (capital and interest) on the local rate and in quality are ranked only slightly below Government securities. There is no recorded case of a British Local Authority defaulting on its obligations and in the event of such a possibility arising it is unlikely that the Government would allow it to happen. From a national point of view it is desirable that Local Authority loans should enjoy one of the highest rankings

CLASSES OF FIXED INTEREST SECURITIES

amongst investors for only so can Local Authorities hope to raise money as and when they need it on the cheapest available terms.

The Loans of the larger Local Authorities, London or Birmingham for example, enjoy a very slightly higher rating than the smaller ones where the appeal tends to be more local; but the loans of the largest Local Authorities never enjoy the investment status of a Government security. London County Council's largest outstanding loan is its 3% Consolidated Stock of which there is £26 million in issue. This is very large by Local Authority standards but it is very small by Government standards where the smallest loans are of several hundred million pounds. As the result no Local Authority stock has the free market possessed by the average Government security. This and the slightly inferior quality of their security means that they can always be bought to give higher yields.

Some idea of comparable yields on Government securities and on Local Authority stocks can be obtained from the following comparison:

Name of Stock	Price	Gross %	Net %
3% Treasury Stock	33	9 3 6	5 7 9
London County 3% Consol. Stock	30¾	9 14 6	5 14 3

Yield at middle market price

The illustration serves to show that Local Authority Stocks have their own rating slightly below that of Government stocks. Whether the rating should be so much lower is open to question. It is inconceivable that in any circumstances the London County Council would default on its obligations and for the superior marketability of 3% Treasury Stock, the reduced yields of 11s. gross and 6s. 6d. net would appear to be large sacrifices to make.

Apart from the publicly quoted loans of Local Authorities, many Local Authorities are prepared to accept loans from institutions and individuals for fixed periods varying from a few days to 25 or more years, usually at interest rates that remain unaltered during the currency of the loans. These rates of interest are slightly higher than those available on the publicly quoted loans but as an offset to this the loans suffer the disadvantage of being unmarketable. If the holder wishes to realize his investment before the fixed maturity date, he can only do so by finding another buyer, and this he may not be able to do without a considerable sacrifice in price. Unlike the quoted stocks stamp duty is payable on transfers. The loans are therefore only for those investors who are prepared to remain frozen in the investment for a period of time.

Public Boards and the Stocks of Water Works Companies

These consist mainly of the stocks of Water and Harbour Boards but also include the stocks of the Port of London Authority, the North of Scotland Hydro Electric Board and the Debenture stocks of the Agricultural Mortgage Corporation. In quality they are to be compared with the stocks of Local Authorities to which in some respects they are related.

The more interesting stocks within this group are the stocks of Water Works. Formed under Acts of Parliament the companies operating the water works are local monopolies. Although in most cases the capital of the companies consists of Debentures, Preference and Ordinary stocks, Ordinary dividends are limited to a maximum which in most cases has been reached. The Ordinary stocks are therefore in the strictest sense Fixed Interest securities, with in some cases (where the maximum dividend has not been reached) the possibility of further modest increases in interest.

The stocks are interesting because of the high yields which they offer—yields which theoretically are insecure but which can be regarded as fairly safe in practice because of the monopoly positions occupied by the companies. Investors would however be unwise to make purchases without carefully studying the earnings and divided circumstances of the particular companies in whose stocks they are thinking of investing.

Loans and Debenture Stocks of Commercial and Industrial Companies

The quality of these depends in large part on the quality of the company, whether its earnings are stable, expanding or contracting and on the relation of the Loan or Debenture interest requirements to the earnings of the company. The difference between a Debenture and a Loan of a company is the difference between a loan, the capital of which is secured on the assets of the company and one the capital of which is not so secured. The difference may be of considerable importance from the investor's point of view, where the company is weak financially, but in the case of a strong well-established company, the real security behind its Loans as well as its Debentures is its earning power. If the company has the earning power it will have no difficulty in raising further Loans or Debentures to repay existing ones. If not, its securities whether they are called Loans or Debentures will not enjoy a high rating amongst investors. None the less Debenture stocks and especially senior or first Debenture stocks will always command premiums over Loan stocks in the same companies and rightly so. The circumstances of a company can change and do change over the years. Investors therefore when making purchases in this field, should examine carefully the quality of the investment from this standpoint.

The first consideration then in assessing the value of a company Loan or Debenture is the quality of the earnings on which the interest payments depend. A company may, it is true, pay interest out of capital but clearly no company will be able to pay interest on its obligations for long when it has ceased to make profits. The type of industry in which the company operates will have to be considered. Where profits are subject to wide fluctuations from year to year, its Loans and Debentures will not enjoy a high rating. Another important factor will be how well Debenture and Loan interest requirements are covered by earnings and whether the Loan or Debenture is a senior Loan or Debenture or a junior one, i.e. one which ranks ahead of all others for capital and interest or one which ranks second or lower. A Loan or Debenture where the interest is covered five or six times by profits and where the company's profits have shown reasonable stability or growth in the past might be considered a sound one. On the other hand if neither of these conditions is satisfied there will be reason to question the suitability of the investment.

Every investment has its price and it may be argued that a high yielding Loan or Debenture stock has its own particular attractions. That is true, but to the extent that it is true, the Loan or Debenture stock is to be considered as an Ordinary stock rather than as a Loan or Debenture. To take an extreme example: suppose a company has fallen on evil days and has ceased to pay interest on its Debenture stock. (This type of situation has been very common in the past although it is much less common today.) Then the stock will not in the strictest sense be a Debenture stock although it will continue to be classified as one, but will be akin more to an Ordinary stock, and subject to the hazards of an Ordinary stock; for the investor no longer has a fixed income.

A Loan or Debenture stock confers on the holder no voting rights at the meetings of the company, except where the interest payments are in default or where the business of the meeting (unusually) involves alteration of the rights of the Loan or Debenture stock holders.

The best method of assessing the earnings cover of Loan or Debenture interest is exemplified as follows. Where a company has profits amounting to £1,000,000 and it has outstanding two Debenture stocks—a First Debenture stock the annual interest on which is £100,000 and a Second Debenture stock the annual interest on which is £150,000—then the interest on the First Debenture stock will absorb 10% of the profits and the interest on the Second Debenture stock a further 15% making 25% of the profits altogether. In other words earnings can fall by 90% before the interest on the First Debenture stock ceases to be fully covered, but only by 75% before the interest on the Second Debenture stock is affected—as follows:

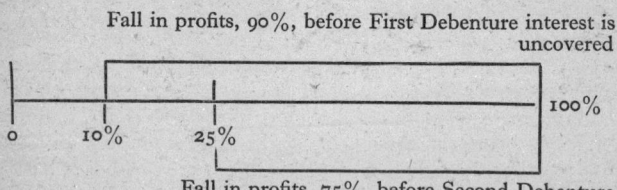

Fall in profits, 90%, before First Debenture interest is uncovered

| 0 | 10% | 25% | | 100% |

Fall in profits, 75%, before Second Debenture interest is uncovered

When Debenture stocks are issued, provision is often made for a Cumulative Sinking Fund to repay the stocks by annual

CLASSES OF FIXED INTEREST SECURITIES 63

drawings over a period of years. Alternatively Debenture stocks may as in the case of Government and Local Authority Loans be redeemable in whole after a specific number of years or they may be perpetual. Interest is always cumulative, i.e. if it is not paid in any one year or series of years, it remains as a debt until it is subsequently paid.

One class of Debenture stock which has become more popular is the Convertible Debenture stock, i.e. the Debenture stock which confers a right on the holder to convert his holding into Ordinary shares or stocks at prices fixed at the time of the issue. The prices fixed are above the current prices of the Ordinary shares or stocks. Such Debenture stocks are particularly suitable for the cautious investor who wants safety of capital and income and yet would like to obtain some advantage from a future rise in the profits of the company.

Preference Stocks

Preference stocks unlike Loan or Debenture stocks are part of the capital of the company. As dividends may not, except in very special circumstances, be paid out of capital the security of a Preference stock, certainly so far as the dividend is concerned, depends entirely on the earnings of the company.

Preference stocks may be cumulative—that is, if dividends are not paid in any one year they must be carried forward as a charge on the earnings of future years and paid before any dividend or return of capital on the Ordinary or other lower ranking capital can be paid; or they may be non-cumulative, that is, if not paid in any one year, the amount unpaid will not be paid out of the profits of future years. They may also be redeemable but usually they are irredeemable.

As a class of security, Preference stocks are not generally popular. Although they form part of the capital of a company they usually have no voting rights unless the company falls on evil times and fails to pay their dividends or wishes to alter their rights. They lack the security of a Debenture stock and have none of the merits of an Ordinary stock. For a non-Cumulative Preference stock there is practically nothing to be said unless the circumstances of the company are such as to make any future failure of dividend extremely improbable. Nor has a Redeemable Preference stock any merits that are not better met from the investor's point of view by a Debenture stock.

Because they do not enjoy the high ranking of Debenture stocks, Preference stocks ought to provide higher yields as a class than other classes of Fixed Interest securities. Owing however, to the effects of corporation tax, this is no longer the case, where the dividends are well covered by profits. Companies have to pay corporation tax on the profits out of which Preference dividends are paid. As the result the dividends may be treated as income on which corporation tax has been paid, that is, as franked investment income, by companies such as investment and insurance companies which are liable to pay corporation tax. The interest on Debenture stocks is not franked, as Debenture interest is a charge against profits before arriving at the amount on which corporation tax has to be paid. Nor is any other interest franked investment income. Preference dividends have therefore an outstanding quality compared with all other classes of Fixed Interest securities which has placed them on a lower yield basis relative to their intrinsic worth, than other Fixed Interest securities and rendered them even less suitable as investments to the private investor who does not pay corporation tax.

In general, Preference shares or stocks are not a satisfactory mode of investment. They lack the safety of a Debenture stock and offer none of the opportunities of an Ordinary stock. They have attractions only where they have been overlooked and the profits out of which the dividend is paid are ample and secure—see method of assessing earnings cover on page 62. But otherwise they would be best avoided by the ordinary investor especially where the dividends are non-cumulative.

Foreign Bonds

There is an extensive list of Foreign Government securities, mostly with chequered histories, which are quoted regularly on the London Stock Exchange. They are Sterling securities in that although they are obligations of Foreign Governments, the capital and the interest of the securities are both expressed in Sterling. Many of them are in default with their interest payments and have been so for years. They are therefore of very little interest to investors except as speculations of a rather doubtful kind.

Yet there may be occasions when the investor will wish to invest in a Foreign Government security of a quality akin to the security provided by his own Government. He may want to do so because he is not very certain about the future course of Sterling but has, for example, faith in the future value of the Dollar. Then he may buy American Government Bonds. They will not be attractive to him as a permanent investment because most American Government Bonds are short-dated securities. None the less as temporary holdings, pending the discovery of satisfactory long-term investments, they may serve a useful purpose.

CHAPTER VII

ORDINARY SHARES AND STOCKS —GENERAL

Description

The Ordinary Share Capital represents the ownership of the company. In this respect it is quite different from Debenture Capital which is loan capital and from Preference Capital which is loan capital in all but name. The holders of the Ordinary shares appoint the Directors who manage the company. The capital of the company belongs to them in proportion to the shares which they hold. The profits belong to them on the same basis and equally, if losses are made, the losses are theirs subject to one important limitation; the Ordinary shareholder cannot lose more than he has already invested in the company or contracted to invest in the company. Under the limited liability provisions of the Companies Act, shareholders have no responsibilities for the debts of the company, in which they have invested money, over and above the amounts of capital they have already subscribed and may have contracted to subscribe in the future. Usually when a company offers shares it requires so much of the cost of the shares to be paid on application by the investor (if they are £1 shares issued at £1, say 5s.), so much on allotment when the shares are issued to the investor (say another 5s.), and the remainder at a later stage when the company calls for it. In the vast majority of cases the company calls for the final payment shortly after the allotment is made, and the shares then become "fully paid" without further liability. Holders of such shares have no further liability for the debts of the company in the event of it going into liquidation and being unable to pay its debts in full. On the other hand holders of shares where there is still a call outstanding, that is where the shares are not "fully paid", have a further liability limited to the amount of the call unpaid.

Most shares dealt in on the London Stock Exchange are fully paid shares. The main exceptions are Bank and Insurance shares, where some uncalled liabilities remain. In these cases, however, the amounts of the uncalled liabilities are usually small in relation to the full market value of the shares, owing to the substantial rises in the prices of shares that have taken place, since their original issue. There is a slight prejudice amongst investors against shares with uncalled liabilities.

When shares become fully paid it is a common practice to convert them into stock, transferable in units of a certain denomination, e.g. £1. This signifies that the shares are fully paid, for there cannot be an uncalled liability on stock.

Companies when they are formed are obliged to fix a nominal value for what is called their Issued Capital, that is to say the capital which has been issued to Shareholders. The amount need not correspond to the real value of the capital employed by the company; but once it is fixed, it must remain fixed until new capital is issued or existing reserves are capitalized. A small stamp duty ($\frac{1}{2}$ of 1%) is payable on the amount so fixed or on the amount of what is called the Authorized Capital if the company has sought power to issue sooner or later more capital than it intends immediately to issue. Companies are also obliged to fix a nominal or par value for their shares. It may be of any amount but the most usual one is £1. How a company's Authorized and Issued Capital appears on its Balance Sheet and its relationship to the total capital employed is illustrated in Appendix VII.

In the past, companies liked to fix a low value for their capitals. This saved stamp duty and it also gave a conservative appearance to their balance sheets. Capital appeared low and reserves appeared high. This factor, plus accumulating profits which are added to reserves, has over the years given the capital accounts of many companies a false appearance. It has also made dividends which are expressed as percentages of nominal capital look high. To remedy this, companies have been obliged in many cases to capitalize their reserves in order to bring the expressed capital into closer line with the real value. The remedy unfortunately gives the impression to some shareholders that they are receiving a capital bonus. They should disabuse their minds of any such notion. The "Capital bonus" gives them nothing that they do not already possess. It merely raises the nominal value of the capital of the company leaving its true value exactly as it was before.

The nearest approach to a remedy would be for companies to adopt the American practice of disregarding, where it exists, the par value of shares when declaring dividends. They would declare so much per share, say 3s. or 3d., instead of so much per cent on the nominal capital. The practice would be made easier if it became permissible (it is at present forbidden by law) to issue, as the Americans do, in many cases, no par shares. This would have advantages for other reasons. Under existing conditions shares have two values—the nominal value to which we have referred and the market value which is the price the investor pays if he wants to buy them. Where the nominal value of a company's capital is low in relation to its true value the market price of the share will stand very much above the nominal value. This is confusing. A share represents a unit of ownership in a company and it has only one real value—the value of the share in the market. The value of the share in the books of the company is of historic interest only and not even of historic interest where the company has deliberately deflated the value of its nominal capital in order to minimize its liability to stamp duty or to give its balance sheet a conservative appearance.

In the event of it becoming common practice in this country to issue no par shares, companies would cease to be able to declare their dividends as so much per cent on the nominal capital; there would be no nominal capital on which to express their dividends. They would have to express their dividends in £ s. d. per share as some companies already do.

In some companies which have Deferred shares in issue there are also shares which are called "Ordinary". But in fact they are not Ordinary shares in the sense we have been discussing because their dividend rights are limited, but Preference, Preferred or Preferred Ordinary shares. It is not therefore by the name that the investor should judge whether the share he is buying is an Ordinary share, but by the rights which attach to it, whether it has full voting rights (and if not, as in the case of recent issues of non-voting Ordinary

ORDINARY SHARES AND STOCKS—GENERAL

shares, it has otherwise the same rights as voting Ordinary shares) and whether it participates fully in the property and profits of the company. Various names by which real Ordinary shares are known, include Deferred shares, Deferred Ordinary shares, Class A shares and Class B shares and, in the United States, Common shares.

The Raising of New Capital

When a company wishes to raise new capital it has the alternative of raising it in the form of Debenture, Preference or Ordinary share capital. If it raises it in either of these forms, it will have to offer the new stock on terms which give buyers a slightly better income return than they would obtain by buying the existing stock in the market. If it decides to issue Debenture or Preference capital it will usually make the issue to the public, but will at the same time send to Ordinary Shareholders special application forms which entitle them to preferential treatment in the allotment of stock for which they apply.

If on the other hand the company decides to issue Ordinary shares it will normally do so and ought to do so on a rights basis. That is to say the issue will be made not to the public but exclusively to existing Ordinary shareholders. This ensures that if the new shares are issued below the market price of the existing shares, as in fact they must be if subscription is to be assured, Ordinary shareholders will be able to subscribe for them fully, or if they do not want to do so they will be able to sell their rights to others, not necessarily existing shareholders, who would like to buy the shares.

The system works as follows. A company with 1,000,000 Ordinary shares of existing capital, wishes to raise £400,000 of new capital. The existing Ordinary shares are £1 shares and stand in the market at £3 per share. The company decides to issue 200,000 new Ordinary shares at £2 per share to existing holders on the basis of 1 new share for every 5 shares held. If in these circumstances the holder wishes to take up the new shares he will subscribe £2 per share, in return for which he will receive the extra shares to which he is entitled. If on the other hand he does not want to add to his present holding, he will sell his rights to the new shares or alternatively sell the new shares nil paid, once the old shares are quoted ex rights. The value of the rights on the old shares and the value of the new shares once the old shares are quoted ex rights will be decided in the following way:

5 shares before the issue is made have a value in the market @ £3 per share of	£15
The issue of each new share increases the company's cash by	2
After the issue 6 shares therefore have a value of .	£17

1 share has a value of $\frac{£17}{6} = 56s.\ 8d.$ The value of the rights on the old share is therefore 3s. 4d., i.e. one-fifth of the difference between what the new share costs (40s.) and what it is worth (56s. 8d.). When the new shares are dealt in, they will be quoted 16s. 8d. nil paid (say 16s. 6d.–16s. 9d.), which is the difference between the adjusted value of the shares and the £2 which the buyer will have to pay before they become fully paid. Because the new shares will be free of transfer stamp to a buyer, until they are fully paid and become registered shares in the ordinary way, they will in practice command a slight premium over the old shares and may therefore be worth say 17s. per share. Henceforth they will vary in price with the price of the old shares, allowance being made only for the amounts that have still to be paid on the shares and for the fact that while they are in scrip (unregistered) form they remain free of stamp.

The methods adopted for the issue of new shares or stock is important from the point of view of Ordinary shareholders. A development of recent origin which Ordinary shareholders are entitled to view with the greatest disfavour is the practice occasionally adopted of issuing convertible Debenture or Loan stocks to the public, by way of an open offer rather than by way of a rights offer. These Debenture or Loan stocks usually carry rights of conversion into Ordinary shares at prices somewhat above the price of the Ordinary shares ruling at the time of issue of the Debenture or Loan stocks. They are tantamount therefore to creating a new potential ownership and to that extent they may reduce the existing Ordinary shareholder's stake in his property. The defence usually offered for the practice is that the sums of capital needed are so large that existing Ordinary shareholders cannot be expected to provide them without inconvenience to themselves. It is not a strong argument in view of the machinery available for selling rights and should be opposed, wherever possible, by Ordinary shareholders.

Reading Company Accounts

As mentioned in an earlier chapter, companies are obliged to make an annual report to their shareholders on their financial progress. The report must include a Balance Sheet showing the assets and liabilities of the company in question, at the end of the period to which the report relates, a Profit and Loss Account showing the profits (or losses) of the company for the year and how they have been employed or will be employed by the company; and if the company has a controlling interest in another or in other companies, a Consolidated Balance Sheet showing the assets and liabilities of the group of companies as a whole. A company has a controlling interest in another company where by virtue of its Ordinary shareholdings in that company it holds more than 50% of the votes. In practice this usually means an Ordinary shareholding of more than 50%. Where, however, there are two classes of Ordinary shares, in all respects similar except that one carries voting rights and the other does not, a more than 50% holding of the former will carry with it control.

The Balance Sheet and Profit and Loss Account and the Report of the Directors which must accompany them, must include, in addition to the information referred to on page 33, details of the main changes in assets during the year, the break-down of turnover between different classes of business, if more than one class is carried on and the profits attributable to each class, the amounts invested in quoted and unquoted investments including the income derived from each together with a report on the main activities of the company. A meeting of Shareholders must be held annually to consider the Report and Accounts and approve them.

Balance Sheets are nowadays presented in many different

ways. The commonest and what might fairly be described as the conventional way of presenting them is to show the assets on the right-hand side and the liabilities on the left-hand side. To many people this is most puzzling since under liabilities is included capital and reserves, items which the normal person would regard not as liabilities but as the balance that remains over after liabilities have been deducted from assets. In fact, however, there is no puzzle—only a misconception of what a company is. A company is a distinct legal person. It owns the assets but it is accountable for these assets first to its creditors and then to its shareholders who own the capital. To a company therefore capital and reserves are a liability although to the people who own the company —the shareholders—they are an asset.

Simple as this explanation may be to some people, it may remain difficult to others and a few companies have accordingly decided to discard the double-entry principles (used in the preparation of their accounts) when they present their balance sheets to their Ordinary shareholders. For this departure from strict orthodoxy there is much to be said because shareholders when they come to review their investments are not interested in the position as seen from the standpoint of the company but in the position as seen from their own standpoint. They want to know what they have invested in the company and if they are to have this presented to them most clearly, then capital will appear not as a liability but as what remains over after all liabilities including capital senior to themselves, i.e. Preference Capital, has been deducted.

We show in Appendix VII what we consider to be a very good example of how to present a Balance Sheet from both the company's and the shareholders' point of view. We also show how these accounts might appear if presented from the shareholder's point of view so that investors who prefer the latter method can convert a conventional Balance Sheet into a form which they understand. Both examples show exactly how much capital the Ordinary shareholders have invested in the company, but one highlights the shareholder's point of view more than the other. They also show how misleading the nominal capital of a company can be as a representation of the amount of capital that is being employed by a company, and, for the same reason, how misleading a dividend expressed in terms of the nominal capital can be.

Figures of capital arrived at in this way do not of course tell shareholders the whole story about their capital. They tell them what the asset value of their capital is according to the Balance Sheet. They do not tell them what its true worth is. First of all, the figures themselves may be partly out of date. Much of the buildings, plant and machinery employed by the company may have been bought very many years earlier when costs were much lower than they are today. If this is so and if the company has not in the meanwhile re-valued its assets, the statement of assets on which the calculation of capital employed is based, may considerably understate the true position. Secondly and more importantly, the true value of a company's capital is not the aggregate value of its assets less its liabilities but the value of its earning power; and that depends on how well the assets have been and are being employed in producing profits.

Even so the asset value figure is interesting and would be still more interesting if it could be supplemented by an estimate of current market asset value. Then it would be possible to compare the rate of profit which the company is making on its assets with the rate of profit being made by other companies in the same type of business and to arrive at conclusions, however tentative, about the efficiency of the management.

The Profit and Loss Account (see Appendix VIII) is the more interesting statement and it is also the easier to understand. It shows, as nearly as they can accurately be calculated, the profits of a company. The chief question mark today surrounds the item of depreciation. Owing to rising costs, the cost of replacing the fixed assets of companies, buildings, plant and machinery, has risen considerably and as a company is a continuing concern it is this replacement cost rather than depreciation on the cost of the old assets that matters to it. To meet this situation, the Board of Trade has made available to manufacturing industries generous grants to cover the cost of installing new plant. For plant or equipment not qualifying for these grants, the Inland Revenue concedes initial (depreciation) allowances of 30% plus annual writing down allowances based on the expected life of the plant or equipment, before determining the profits on which tax has to be paid.

Having arrived at the figure of profit after depreciation there falls to be deducted corporation tax and Debenture interest and Preference dividends, if any. The remaining profits are the profits available for Ordinary dividends. Income tax must be deducted by the company from the interest and dividends when they are paid, and the tax so deducted paid over to the Inland Revenue. From this point onwards, it is possible to calculate the rate of earnings on the company's Ordinary share capital by dividing the earnings available for Ordinary dividends by the gross cost of the dividends and multiplying the result by the rate of Ordinary dividend paid. A more instructive way is however, to extend the system for calculating the earnings cover of Debenture interest discussed in Chapter VI. If, to take the same illustration, the profits of a company after corporation tax are £1,000,000 and in addition to the two Debenture stocks there is Preference capital the service of which requires £50,000 gross and Ordinary capital the gross dividend on which requires £300,000 the division of the company's profits will be as follows:

	%
First Debenture stock	0–10
Second Debenture stock	10–25
Preference stock	25–30
Ordinary stock	30–60
Reserved	60–100

If the dividend on the Ordinary stock is 10% and the price of £1 of stock is £2 the yield on the Ordinary stock will be 5%. To provide this yield however only $\frac{3}{7}$ths of the available profits were used, i.e. 30% to 60% (= 30), out of 30% to 100% (= 70) of the profits. So the dividend was covered $2\frac{1}{3}$ times $\left(\dfrac{70}{30}\right)$ by available earnings, or alternatively the earnings yield of the stock is $2\frac{1}{3} \times 5$ or $11\frac{2}{3}\%$.

Although it is of interest for the investor to know the relationship between earnings and dividends, the practice has developed in recent years, of quoting price-earnings ratios instead of earnings yields. Price-earnings ratios are the

ORDINARY SHARES AND STOCKS—GENERAL

number of times the earnings yield must be multiplied to reach 100. It follows therefore that the earnings yield can be calculated by reversing the operation, i.e. by finding the number of times the price-earnings ratio must be multiplied to reach 100. In the above illustration, the price-earnings ratio is 8·6. A low price-earnings ratio therefore indicates a high earnings yield and conversely.

In addition to the fact that the table (the priority percentages as they are called) when taken in conjunction with the yield on the Ordinary dividend enables the investor to calculate the relationship of earnings to dividend in two ways, it also enables him to see at a glance how marginal the earnings belonging to the Ordinary stockholders are. In this case the first 30% of profits belong to the Debenture and Preference stockholders and the remaining 70% to the Ordinary stockholders. If in these circumstances profits were to fall by 50%, the entire 50% would come out of the 70% share belonging to Ordinary stockholders whose earnings in the result would be reduced not by 50% but by $\frac{50}{70} \times 100\%$ or by 71·4%. The advantages would be correspondingly greater for Ordinary stockholders if profits were to rise. Accordingly where the investor fears that profits may fall in the future, he will be wary of Ordinary stocks which rank for dividend only after substantial payments have been made in respect of Debenture interest and Preference dividends. Equally when he expects profits to rise he will be particularly interested in such stocks for then every proportionate increase in total profits will mean a proportionately greater increase in the profits attributable to the Ordinary stockholders.

We shall refer again to this question of gearing as it is called in Chapter X, pages 103 to 105.

Yields

As we have seen, Ordinary shares differ from Fixed Interest securities in one important particular. Whereas Fixed Interest securities are entitled to a fixed annual income which under normal conditions is paid regularly each year, Ordinary shares have no such right. Their incomes are liable to change from year to year in accordance with changes in the profits from which they are paid. Ordinary share yields which are based on dividends which have already been paid have therefore very much less significance than Fixed Interest security yields. As the prices of all securities are conditioned not by the dividends that have been paid but by the dividends that are considered likely to be paid in the future, the effect of this is to make comparisons of yields between Ordinary shares and Fixed Interest securities misleading.

In the past it has been usual for Ordinary shares to yield more than Preference stocks and Debenture stocks in the same company except where there were special grounds for supposing that Ordinary dividends were about to be increased. The reason for this was that Ordinary dividends were paid out of the least secure part of a company's profits, that the amounts paid in Ordinary dividends represented the best estimate at the time of what a company could afford to pay out of its then known profits and that there was no assurance that profits in the future would increase. Today, according to one school of thought the latter two conditions no longer apply. Companies provide internally out of reserved profits a large proportion of their growing capital needs and this capital earns future profits; and Government policy is now directed everywhere, even at the risk of a moderate degree of inflation, to making the fullest use of available manpower, available capital and available inventiveness. As the result the national income is bound to rise and with it profits and existing capital's share of these profits.

The theory is an interesting one and if it is right justifies the placing of Ordinary shares as a class on a permanently lower yield basis than other classes of securities. Unfortunately, however, it overlooks the possibility that if as a consequence of the pursuit of full employment, inflation should persist, company profits and dividends become an easy and legitimate target for the tax collector. When effective competition ceases, as it does under conditions of inflation, the system of private enterprise loses one of its most valuable attributes, the presentation of a choice to the customer, to accept or not accept the quality of the product offered and pay or not pay the price asked. If he will not accept or not pay, there will always be others who will, which will force

ORDINARY SHARES AND STOCKS—GENERAL

him in the end to join the queue. The pursuit of efficiency suffers with the disappearance of the need to do so and the pursuit of profits by any means, takes over. No Government with a mandate based on popular support can accept this. Profits and dividends must be curbed if inflation cannot be ended by other means.

Apart from this, the theory also depends on whether the trade cycle which is rooted in human psychology has finally been conquered and on whether society will be prepared indefinitely to accept the discomforts and distortions of inflation as the economic framework of their lives. On the prospects of these, more will be said in a later chapter. Should, however, the answer be favourable, it will not follow as a consequence that Ordinary shares will in all cases and at all times provide the safest medium of investment. Different companies and different industries will face different circumstances and the companies and industries which investors select as the favourites of today may not turn out to be the successes of tomorrow. Then again, the prices of Ordinary shares as a whole may themselves rise to levels which more than allow for all the favourable developments that will occur for many years to come and none of the disappointments proceeding, perhaps, from internal political or external economic causes. The danger of this will be the greater, the more investors allow profit expectations in the future (which there can be no satisfactory means of measuring), as distinct from performance in the present, to influence share prices. Investors buying at these prices may in the result lose large amounts of their capital. For this reason, they would be well advised, should these conditions ever arise, to consider carefully the future dividend increases that must occur, if they are ultimately to receive from an investment in Ordinary shares, the same income that they will receive from an equal investment in sound Fixed Interest securities. Then at least they will have some idea of the risks involved in the prices they are paying.

CHAPTER VIII

BRITISH ORDINARY SHARES AND STOCKS

By British Ordinary shares and stocks we mean the Ordinary shares and stocks of United Kingdom companies or of Overseas companies, such as South African gold-mining companies in which there are substantial United Kingdom interests and whose shares are dealt in regularly on the London Stock Exchange—with a few exceptions in fact the shares and stocks which are quoted in the Stock Exchange Daily Official List.

The Effects of Post-War Inflation

The British economy has ever since the war been wrestling with the problem of inflation and the attendant problem of selling sufficient of its goods abroad to pay for the goods it has had to import. Successive Governments have attempted to solve the problem but, until recently, with little success. The Socialist Government which took office immediately after the war largely created the problem by its failure to recognize the full extent of the material losses the country had suffered in the war, by its fear of the return of depression and unemployment after the main post-war shortages had been made good, and by its consequent emphasis on spending policies. The school age was raised before the schools had been built and the teachers provided to cope with the increased numbers of schoolchildren. Expensive housing standards were laid down for the many new houses that had to be built which, desirable as they were in themselves, were out of keeping with the nation's straitened circumstances. An ambitious and comprehensive National Health Service was embarked on and meanwhile much had to be done to repair the physical damage caused by the war and to build up adequate reserves of goods and materials. Complicating matters for the Socialist Government, the American Government summarily ended Lend-Lease, the arrangement whereby the country had secured free of charge many of its essential war-time supplies from the United States. In spite of this, war-time controls were kept in being to prevent prices from rising and artificially cheap money was encouraged to assure a plentiful demand for whatever was available. Taxation was kept high, effectively removing any chances that there might have been of a revival in private saving.

Gradually the nature of the inflation that was taking place became apparent to the Government. This it attempted to deal with, not by setting prices free to rise or by curbing the supply of money but by still higher taxation, and by dividend limitation to force companies to increase their saving. The measures were not enough by themselves to deal with the problem, partly for the reason that without an adequate control of the supply of money (which by its insistence on cheap money and in particular cheap Government borrowing it was eschewing) too much money remained in circulation, and partly for the reason that they failed to command the confidence of the people in whose hands the management of the still very important private sector of the economy lay. Nothing promotes inflation so much as lack of confidence in the ability or integrity of those in whose hands the primary responsibility for managing money lies and there was little confidence in the financial policies of the Socialists.

Yet the Socialist Government if it failed to check inflation had some success in restraining it. True the pound had to be devalued. But in the opinion of many, devaluation was unnecessary at the time. The pound at $4 to the pound was not overvalued in terms of what it could buy at home. Devaluation was forced on the Government mainly because it failed to establish confidence at home and abroad in its ultimate ability to stop inflation, and because of the distrust it engendered by its unfriendly attitude towards private capital. In spite of controls, money was able to leave the country. Because of controls and of the fear of an ultimate devaluation, foreigners were reluctant to leave money in the country longer than was necessary; and where they had payments to make, they were anxious to postpone making them for as long as possible in the hope of acquiring sterling cheaper at a later stage. In the result the country found itself in heavy deficit with its dollar payments and a devaluation of the pound from $4·03 to $2·80 seemed the only way out in the Autumn of 1949.

If those in whose hands the management of the private sector of the economy lay were wanting in enthusiasm for Socialist financial methods, they were in large measure obedient to the Government's dictates. Without statutory support and on mere instructions from the Government they limited dividends. Between 1946 and 1950, when the Socialists were in power, total company profits rose from the region of £1,850 million to the region of £2,850 million. Of this increase of £1,000 million or 54%, taxes absorbed £410 million, company saving £570 million and interest and dividends a mere £20 million. Ordinary dividends rose by rather more than interest and dividends as a whole, owing to a fall in interest and Preference dividends. Their increase over the period was limited however to £47 million or to 13% of the 1946 total and most of this increase occurred in the period 1946 to 1948.

Since 1950, and particularly since the return to power of a Conservative Government in 1951, there has been a considerable improvement in the position of Ordinary shareholders. Between 1950 and 1957 company profits rose by a further £1,430 million. Of this increase taxes absorbed £405 million and company saving £516 million. The balance of £509 million was absorbed by interest and dividends, of which the Ordinary shareholder's portion was £312 million. The rise in the cost of interest and Preference dividends was explained by the raising of new capital and by the sharp rise in interest rates which occurred over the period. The rise in Ordinary dividends, which was in the region of 75%, was explained partly by the raising of new capital but very largely by the raising of dividends.

Dividend increases of such an order over so short a period must be construed as a most satisfactory result and as testimony to the investment merits of Ordinary shares. To see the position in its true perspective one has however to consider the history not only of the six years from 1950 to 1957 but also the history of the whole period covering the years immediately before the war, the war years and the early post-war years. Taking 1938 as the starting point the National Income increased from £4,816 million to £17,604 million in 1957 or by over 250%. During the same period Ordinary dividends rose from £360 million to £715 million, or by slightly less than 100%. On that basis Ordinary dividends did not keep pace with national growth. Nor did they even keep pace with the cost of living, which rose by more than 150%.

Better experience may yet be in store for Ordinary shares. If dividends have not kept pace with the growth in the National Income, profits have. Company profits were estimated in 1938 to amount to £1,026 million. By 1957 they had risen to an estimated £4,233 million or to over 300% above their 1938 level. These are gross figures, before charging depreciation, and do not therefore take account of the greatly increased cost of replacing capital today, but they do indicate that companies could pay much larger dividends than they are at present paying. The increase in wages over the same period was from £1,920 million to £7,720 million, an increase of 300%.

The following table abstracted from the Central Statistical Office's publication, *National Income and Expenditure*, 1957, gives some idea of the possibilities of further dividend increases on the basis of existing profits without making allowance for any improvement in the future level of profits.

		1938		1957
			£ million	
Total Profits			1,026	4,233
Less Debenture Interest and Preference Dividends, etc.	248		422	
Depreciation	142		748	
Remittances abroad	33		231	
United Kingdom Taxes	95	518	1,122	2,523
Net Profits			508	1,710
Ordinary Dividends			360	715
Ratio of Net Profits to Dividends			1·4	2·4
Ordinary Dividends if pre-war ratio maintained representing rise of 70% over the 1957 rate of £715 million				1,200

The Value of Ordinary Shares

During the ten years following 1958, profits before taxation continued to increase and dividends with them. As the result, however, of the change in the system of taxation in 1965—the introduction of corporation tax—much of the increase in profits which might have been expected to accrue to the benefit of Ordinary shareholders has been absorbed by the Government. The old relationship between profits and dividends has in the event been restored, but at the expense of a very considerable increase in the Government's share. There has also been a complete reversal of the traditional relationship between the yields on Ordinary dividends and the yields on Fixed Interest securities. Prices at the beginning of the period were low and much of the early rise was justified by this consideration alone. Latterly, however, all caution seemed to be thrown overboard, spurred in part by the conviction that inflation had come finally to stay and partly by the belief that the risk had been taken out of Ordinary share investment by the combined effects of inflation and the spread of investment (discussed in Chapter X) made readily available through the growth of the Unit Trust movement. No consideration whatsoever was given to the rapidly deteriorating economic position of the country and there was a time even when bad and good economic news alike were construed as favourable to the future of Ordinary shares.

The devaluation of sterling in November 1967 and the wrong deductions that were made from it, were largely responsible for these developments. Devaluation was the easy way, or so it appeared, to restore the competitiveness of British exports, but when this was construed as evidence of government weakness and the probable preliminary to further devaluations, the Government was forced, as money continued to flow out of the country, to take really tough action both through the Budget and through the control which the Bank of England exercises on the supply of money. It was action which should have been taken at a much earlier stage, when less toughness might have sufficed. It was action which when once taken was bound to have serious repercussions on the prices of Ordinary shares and on investment generally.

To place all of the responsibility on the Government for what went wrong would be unfair. Clearly it had the main responsibility. Part must, however, be assumed by those in charge of the country's financial markets and the way in which these markets are organized. There is a proneness to serious exaggeration capable of having calamitous consequences if not checked in time. No Government is able alone to manage the economy without the rational support of all the elements which go to make it up. This support it has not had, and for lack of it, it may have been forced to take more drastic action than was strictly necessary.

A feature of markets in recent years has been the take-over bid. These happen when an individual (or company) sees ways, or believes he does, of converting some or all of the assets of a company to new uses which will have the effect of increasing earning power and the dividends a company can pay. They were particularly appropriate in the early years after the war when, due to investors' despondency, the shares of many of the leading companies could be purchased at prices corresponding to less than the worth of their net liquid assets and on the basis of earning yields of 20% and upwards and dividend yields considerably higher than those available on Fixed Interest securities. It is a different matter when, in conditions completely the reverse, large companies enter the field, risking the money of their shareholders, to buy control of rival companies and sometimes of other companies at prices which cannot conceivably be justified except on the basis of the most optimistic forecasts of future earnings over a long period of years.

For the shareholder in the company taken over, there is no reason for particular concern, as unless he has a special attachment to the company, he usually receives a generous price sufficient to compensate him for his loss of expectations, coupled with an option to enter the new partnership if he wishes to do so. But for the shareholder of the taxing-over company, there is no effective choice. He is not in a position to judge the merits of the new proposal and even if he is, he is unlikely to carry his way with other shareholders against the combined opinion of the Board of Directors. Nor can the taking-over companies really know what is involved until the amalgamation is complete, for it is in the nature of take-overs that they are battles and not a coming together of minds, with a mutual sharing of information, in the hope that it may be advantageous to both sides to go ahead with the union.

Where an individual risks his capital in a take-over, that is his affair, although the public interest may be involved. Where, however, a company does the taking-over, where therefore there is no longer the same element of individual risk to give pause to an un-wise decision, wider issues are involved which seem to point to the need for a much greater degree of public scrutiny than is now available. It is not without interest that whereas in earlier times when Ordinary shares were transparently undervalued, the individual was the prime mover, in recent times, with Ordinary shares already more than fully valued by all the conventional methods of appraising values—extremely high interest rates side by side with exceptionally low Ordinary share yields, the consequence of inflation—the prime mover has been the company.

Ordinary shares carry risks not attaching to Fixed Interest securities. They also provide opportunities for increasing income not possessed by Fixed Interest securities. What a company is expected to earn and pay out in dividends, decides its value but only in relation to what might be earned by the same outlay of funds in another field. When the yields offered by Ordinary shares are extremely low when compared with what may be earned by the outlay of the same funds in well secured Fixed Interest securities, when no one in his senses could ever believe that a British government would be foolish enough or dishonest enough to default on its debt obligations, when the cause of the disparity in yields is inflation, which because of the immense damage it is doing to the country's economic life, the Government is doing everything to end, and when the country happens to be the United Kingdom, the most secure parliamentary democracy in the world with a government which can soon be changed if it fails, the investor in the fully exposed position of backing inflation all the way may be forgiven if he asks—is it wise?

Types of British Ordinary Shares

By no means all of the shares actively dealt in on the London Stock Exchange are subject to the economic and political risks peculiar to the United Kingdom. The London Stock Exchange as we have seen deals actively in the shares of many companies whose business is predominantly overseas—South

African gold-mining shares, the shares of the world's principal diamond mines, Rhodesian copper shares, Malayan tin shares, Australian lead and zinc shares and Far Eastern rubber and tea shares. In many of these cases the companies are domiciled outside the United Kingdom and are not therefore subject to British taxation or to regulations which might in the future affect dividends. Moreover the influences affecting their profits are world influences rather than purely British influences; the price of gold is determined by the American fixed buying price of $35 per ounce and the relationship between the South African rand (formerly the pound) and the dollar, the price of copper by the demand for it which is universal—and so with the prices of lead, zinc, rubber, tea and diamonds.

The main influences affecting oil and shipping shares may also be said to be world ones. The chief companies are however domiciled in the United Kingdom and are, therefore, apart from their general dependence on world economic conditions, British concerns, subject to British taxation and British influences regarding dividends.

Otherwise the main classes of Ordinary shares dealt in on the London Stock Exchange are the shares of British companies domiciled in the United Kingdom with their predominant interests in the United Kingdom. As we saw in Chapter III the list of companies and industries is long and the interests and risks varied. One company may operate in several industries. Companies in the same industry may concentrate on the home market and the export market in widely different proportions. They may have all their manufacturing facilities concentrated in the United Kingdom although they are large exporters or they may handle their foreign trade mainly through the agency of foreign subsidiaries or foreign producing plants. There are companies catering for almost every type of consumer interest on the production side, including:

> Flour, sugar, bread, canned foods, mustard and starches, milk products, medicines, chemicals, alcoholic drinks, tobacco, household equipment and furniture, clothing, motor cars, radio and television, paper, cosmetics, soap, margarine, cotton rayon and wool, textile fabrics and sewing threads.

And on the distribution side:

> Grocery chains, drapers and general merchandisers, caterers and hoteliers.

There are companies engaged mainly in the business of managing money—banks, bill discounting companies, hire purchase companies, insurance companies, financial trusts, investment companies and unit trusts.

There are companies manufacturing almost every type of capital equipment, including building and constructional engineering—boilers, steam engines, turbines, diesel engines, electrical switch gear, ball bearings, electrical generators, cables, electronic equipment, business machines, motor and aircraft engines, motor lorries, ships and aircraft, steel and a wide range of metal products.

Included in these companies and industries there are companies and industries whose export markets, if they are not so important as their domestic markets, are at least of major importance. This is true of the motor-car and electrical equipment industries which are now two of our major exporting industries, and of the manufacturers of cotton and woollen goods, and of the makers of boilers and a wide variety of other engineering goods.

The industry in which a company operates naturally affects its rating in the eyes of the investor. The industries which produce the steadiest incomes are certain consumer industries such as breweries and tobacco. In good times and in bad times beer and tobacco consumption vary less than most other items of consumption, and competition is not strong either because, as in the case of some breweries, they dominate certain local markets or because they sell well-known products for which the demand has become established. Much the same is true of the wheat-milling, sugar-refining, distilling and mustard and starch industries which are controlled by a few leading companies. The same should be true of the soap and margarine industry which is dominated by one company, Unilever Limited. This company, in association with its partner Unilever N.V., has however many other interests—raw material interests, interests in retail distribution not connected with either soap or margarine and vast overseas manufacturing and producing interests which place it in a special category of its own.

The shares of companies which cater for the basic needs of the home consumer are generally safer than the shares of companies which manufacture capital equipment, but they are not necessarily better shares from the investor's point of view. It all depends on the type of consumer share and on the type of capital equipment share. The shares of companies engaged in distribution are on the whole safe but dull, with some well-known exceptions such as Woolworths and Marks and Spencer where dynamic management has produced over the years and continues to produce exceptional growth of profits and dividends. As a general rule industries and companies within industries must be selected by the investor with a particular regard for the future prospects of the industries and the quality of the managements within the industries. Time was when the capital equipment industries as a class were exposed to severe cyclical changes in their fortunes. When trade was depressed and the supply of existing equipment was more than sufficient to cope with such trade as there was, few industries were interested in spending money on new equipment. Conditions are different now but whether the change is permanent or temporary will depend on the continued success of full employment policies. Logically, considering that three-quarters of the population of the world live under conditions bordering on starvation and well below the levels of normal subsistence, the scope for further capital accumulation, which has done so much in the past to lift the living standards of the western world, should be immense. But human nature operating politically moves in odd ways. Even the enlightened and humane Americans, who in the twenty years since the war have spent immense sums on overseas gifts, have spent them mainly, not on food or capital equipment, of which the backward areas of the world stand in greatest need, but on arms to help them protect their regimes, mostly unprogressive, from being overturned by influences from without.

Leaving aside the future needs of the backward countries there is however scope for the use of more and more capital in industry and it is in this direction mainly that the investor should look for the profits of future growth. The consumer industries will benefit from improving technology but it is the capital goods and the scientific industries such as the chemical and electrical industries which will lead the way. Furthermore, if as a small island community we are to get a living we must be able to sell to other people more and more of the things that they are less fitted to make for themselves. They will always be catching up with us as they have already done in the field of textiles. Our job will be to keep ourselves that one step ahead in efficiency of production.

The textile industries generally do not offer an inviting prospect to investors except on yield considerations (yields are generous) and where new fibres are being developed which replace existing ones. The experience of the rayon industry does not however encourage much optimism from this latter point of view. The rayon industry has shot ahead at the expense of its old rivals but the victory it has secured on the production side has not been matched in the same degree by a victory on the profits side. The advance of rayon has in fact been hotly contested as it was bound to be by the natural fibre industries and more recently by nylon and other synthetic fibres, with the result that profits over the years have advanced only moderately.

There are two main classes of banks whose shares are dealt in on the London Stock Exchange, the joint-stock or clearing banks and the merchant banks. The former as explained on page 40 and the associated Appendix V, occupy a key position in the management of the country's monetary affairs. Their income consists mainly of the difference on the one hand between the interest they earn on loans to industry and private individuals, on investments, mainly short-term Government Securities, on Treasury and other bills of exchange and on short term loans against the security of bills and on the other the interest they pay on money deposited with them. On current deposits, the larger, they pay no interest. On time deposits, the other main component of total deposits, they pay a rate of interest well below the level they can earn on their loans and advances which is usually 1% to 2% above Bank Rate. High interest rates and an expending supply of money, largely created by themselves through the position they occupy in the monetary system, favour their earnings, as low interest rates and a contracting supply of money, depress them. By virtue of the powers which they wield they are, however, very susceptible to the dictates of Government policy as expressed through the Bank of England, to which they must be obedient. Their shares enjoy a fairly high investment status but they can never possess the growth opportunities of the successfully managed merchant bank. These banks have no power to create money. They are dependent on their own resources and on money they can borrow on strict commercial terms. Their main business is to assist in financing new enterprise directly and indirectly through public issues of capital and to advise on the merging of larger undertakings and generally assist them with their financial problems. Most of the merchant banks were until recent years in private hands but a wide choice is now available to the investing public. Yields, reflecting the growth potentials, are generally low but for those to whom immediate income is not important and who can afford to wait, the shares of the leading banks are worth consideration.

Bill discount companies or discount houses are the main specialists in Treasury Bills. Their principal business is, with the aid of call money provided by the banks, to finance the week to week needs of the Government. There are two views about their activities—one that they are a useful buffer between the banks and the Government—the other that now that they no longer conduct a big business in foreign bills, they have become an anachronism. As regards the first, there are good reasons for supposing that the banks with their very much greater resources are capable of assuming by themselves responsibility for financing the Government's needs. To leave it, as is done at present, to the discount houses is to increase considerably the difficulties of controlling credit, for when they get into difficulties, as they often do in periods of credit stringency, the Bank of England has to help them out, thereby largely nullifying the effects of the stringency which it is Government policy to create.

Hire purchase companies are engaged in the business of providing finance for the purchase by consumers of durable goods on credit. Their business is growing but as a consequence of Government measures to check inflation, it has been subject in recent years to frequent and embarrassing interruptions. The shares of the leading companies offer high yields for an Ordinary share, reflecting the unsettled political conditions under which they operate.

The most interesting and over the years one of the most profitable fields of investment has been insurance. Four main branches of insurance are represented in the shares of the leading companies—Life, Fire, Accident and Marine. The yields on insurance shares are generally low for life companies but are a good deal larger for companies engaged in the other classes of insurance business where underwriting experience has been much less satisfactory in recent years. The main sources of income are insurance or underwriting profits and investment income. Underwriting profits are liable to fluctuate from year to year, but over the years the trend has been upwards in accordance with the expanding character of the business.

The more important element in profits is investment income and this, in reflection of steadily rising premium incomes, rises steadily from year to year. As it is out of investment income that insurance companies usually pay their dividends, this was a considerable source of strength in the past when underwriting profits were also rising. It is of less importance today with underwriting profits turning downwards and often showing losses. General insurance business has certainly become more hazardous in recent years removing much of the certainty of growth on which investors used to be able with confidence to rely.

Some insurance companies transact only life business. Life assurance, which combines pension annuities and other types of annuity business, is one of the most rapidly growing branches of insurance. Share yields are usually low but growth of income has in the past been steady and shows every likelihood of continuing to be so in the future.

CHAPTER IX

THE ORDINARY SHARES AND COMMON STOCKS OF OTHER COUNTRIES

These shares or stocks divide themselves naturally into two broad classes—the shares or stocks of foreign countries and the shares or stocks of Commonwealth countries including Canada, which although a member of the Commonwealth is not a member of the Sterling Area.

Foreign Shares and Stocks

In practice this means the Common stocks of American companies. Most countries outside Russia and her satellites have their own Security markets in which it is possible to operate from London. Language differences, currency complications and political considerations, however, place their securities out of bounds to the ordinary investor who wants to know what he is buying and why he is buying it. In a few cases (the Royal Dutch Company and Unilever N.V., another Dutch company and partner of Unilever Limited, are two examples that come to mind) the companies may be of sufficient international importance to have as, or nearly as, active a market in London as in their country of origin. But otherwise, the shares of foreign companies, other than those of the United States, are better left to the specialists who know what they are doing and whose business it is to study the political economic and currency conditions of the countries in whose markets they operate.

There are several considerations which, taken together, establish a powerful case in favour of some interest by British investors in American Common stocks.

(1) The Americans are an English-speaking people. Information about American industries and companies is as readily available to British investors as it is to American investors, with, in these days of fast communications, very little extra delay.

(2) The Americans as a people are greedy for information. There is therefore a more than ample supply of information available to anyone who wishes to read about the aspects of the American economy which concern the investor, both about industries and about companies.

(3) The Americans are ardent believers in the system of free and private enterprise. The Labour Party is weak and ineffective, and the Trade Unions although strong and well organized are tied to no political party. They lean generally towards the Democratic Party, one of the two main parties, which in outlook is to be compared with the former Liberal Party of this country before the rise of the Labour Party.

(4) The economy is the largest and richest in the world. It is virtually self supporting and yet imports more and exports more than any other country. Between one-third and a half of the Western world's output of raw materials is produced and consumed in the United States, so that what is happening in the United States is of great economic importance to the rest of the world.

(5) The dollar is the world's leading currency and occupies a position similar to that which the pound used to occupy. It is supported by a strong world trading position and by a gold reserve fully equal to the responsibilities which it has assumed. The price of gold is based on the American dollar.

American Common stocks are, in all material respects, the American counterparts of British Ordinary shares. American corporations, the name by which their companies are generally known, are limited liability companies controlled by their Common stockholders in the same manner as British limited companies are controlled by their Ordinary shareholders. In one important respect Common stocks are superior to British Ordinary shares. Because the Americans believe in the virtues of private enterprise, there has been no attempt by the Government or by Labour to dictate to corporations how they are to use their profits when made. Competition renders profits less stable, but once they are made, corporations are free to distribute them without let or hindrance in any way they choose.

SHARES AND STOCKS OF OTHER COUNTRIES 93

The 1965 Finance Act brought British company taxation more or less into line with American company taxation. It also ended the double tax relief which British investors were previously able to claim against the corporation profits tax paid by American companies. The dividends they receive from American common stocks now bear the full rate of corporation profits tax and in addition a 15% withholding tax. This latter tax has its counterpart in a tax of the same amount which, under an agreement between the British and American Governments, is imposed by the British Government on dividends paid by British companies to American shareholders. Under the agreement each Government undertakes to grant relief in respect of these withholding taxes against the taxes they impose on dividends received from the other country. Thus in the case of an American dividend received by a British holder, the paying agent collecting the dividend, usually a bank, pays 15% to the American Government, converts the balance into sterling, pays the equivalent of 5s. 3d. to the British Inland Revenue, if the standard rate of tax is 8s. 3d. and pays the balance to the holder.

The British investor in American common stocks unfortunately cannot freely buy the stocks. Under existing British exchange regulations he can buy them only if he can find other British residents who are prepared to sell to him, or if he can find a British seller of dollars. In either case, he is liable to have to pay a premium over the American cost price, which has on occasion been as much as 50% but has at other times been negligible and even negative. This latter disadvantage is partially counteracted by the fact that so long as sterling remains a restricted currency, the investor, in buying dollars or dollar securities, is acquiring a currency or titles to a currency which is freely convertible into every other currency and which is generally recognized to be one of the soundest. If therefore he has to pay a premium (and he will only pay a premium under conditions where sterling is weak, or where for other reasons dollar securities appear to have exceptional attractions) he will be receiving something of value in return. The dollar premium (subject to an obligation on the part of the holder to hand over to the exchange authorities 25% of the dollar proceeds at par when he disposes of a stock) is accordingly not to be regarded as an expense of dealing but as part of the price of an American security to a British buyer, which he may or may not be able to recover if and when he sells.

American Common Stocks unlike the majority of British Ordinary shares are bearer stocks. Purchases therefore escape the 1% stamp duty imposed by the British Government on transfers of registered securities other than its own securities and the securities of British Local Authorities and Public Boards. As the result, even allowing for the fact that the purchase of American securities, if made through a London broker, involves the payment of two brokers' commissions, a commission to the London broker and one to the American broker, the expenses of dealing are similar to those of dealing in British Ordinary shares. Nor is there any reason why the purchase should be made through a London broker, unless the investor is specially anxious to have his guidance. Many American Stockbrokers have offices in London from which they are capable of handling business on New York terms.

American Common stocks cover a wider range of industries than British Ordinary shares partly for the reason that the country is much richer in raw material resources and partly for the reason that all enterprise in the United States remains in private hands. Industries in the United States which are in private hands and for which there are no British equivalents are railways or railroads as they are there called, the electric, gas and natural gas supply industries, coal, telephones, and sound radio. On the other hand American industries, where they come directly into competition with British industries, suffer one disadvantage. American labour costs are much higher than British labour costs. Where foreign competition is involved therefore the competitive advantage invariably lies with the British industry. This is particularly true of the shipping and shipbuilding industries.

Straight comparisons between the yields on British Ordinary shares and on American Common stocks are not easy to make. Dividend yields and price-earnings ratios are compiled on a similar basis and it is therefore possible to compare at any one time the level of yields and prices. On the other hand the British investor is obliged to find dollars before he can enter the American investment market and this as we have

SHARES AND STOCKS OF OTHER COUNTRIES

seen can be very expensive, increasing greatly the prices he must pay and reducing considerably the yields he will receive as compared with an American investor in his own market.

Before leaving the subject of American Common stocks, there is one point puzzling to British investors which should be explained. This is the method of quoting the London prices of the stocks. It is difficult to find any rational explanation for the method and it is to be hoped that, in the interests of clarity and simplicity, it will soon be abolished. Meanwhile investors will want to know how it works, and how the London dollar price, which is quoted to them for American securities, relates to the American price. London brokers base their price on a dollar rate of $5 to the £. As the current official rate is $2·40 to the £, they multiply the New York price of a security by 5 and divide the result by 2·40. This gives what they call their London dollar price which when divided by 5 gives the price of the security in sterling. The London price also takes account of the dollar premium. This is allowed for by adding the appropriate percentage, 3%, 5% or 10%, whatever it may be, to the London dollar price. To take an example, suppose the dollar premium is 5% and that the price of a stock in New York is $76, the London dollar price will be calculated as follows:

$$\$76 \times \frac{5}{2\cdot 4} \times \frac{105}{100} = \frac{76 \times 105}{48} = \$166\tfrac{1}{4}$$

The price of $166¼ London, when divided by 5, gives a sterling equivalent price of £33 5s. 0d., which is exactly the same price as would have been obtained by dividing the New York price of 76 by the current exchange rate of 2·40 and multiplying the result by 1·05 to allow for the premium.

It would save a great deal of trouble and avoid a great deal of confusion if brokers adopted a London sterling price. For a price quoted in dollars at a rate of exchange, which has never existed officially, there is no justification.

Within recent years there has been a considerable increase in interest amongst investors in the possibilities of investment in the countries of Western Europe and in the vigorously expanding Japanese economy. A wide range of securities relating to each country is quoted daily in the financial press.

The information publicly available about each investment is however meagre by our standards. Yields tend to be low and the selection of investments if made should be left to specialists with an intimate knowledge of the countries concerned. Individuals with a good knowledge of particular countries may of course be able to make their own selections.

Commonwealth and South African Shares and Stocks

Canada is one of the dollar countries. A neighbour of the United States, Canada has the closest economic connections with both the United States and the United Kingdom. She exports agricultural and forestry products, chiefly wheat, newsprint and woodpulp and a wide range of raw materials including nickel, copper, aluminium, lead, zinc, iron ore, and, recently in increasing quantities, oil and natural gas. The United States values Canada mainly as a nearby and secure source of raw materials and has for this reason supplied a large amount of the capital needed for the development of the country, since the end of the war. Canada has abundant supplies of many of the resources which are gradually being exhausted in the United States. Moreover economic considerations have favoured north-south development between Canada and the United States rather than east-west development along the 3,000-mile frontier, much of it sparsely populated, which separates the two countries.

Canada's abundant supply of natural resources has been an asset of considerable value during the post-war years of booming demand. These conditions could however change very quickly in the event of a world economic setback. American protectionism, never far below the surface, could be quickly turned against Canada as, from time to time, it has been against other foreign countries. Should this happen it would be felt particularly severely by Canada, because of the extent to which she has become dependent upon trade outlets in the American market. Such a setback may never occur, nevertheless it is a risk which should not be overlooked by the investor.

Industries which stand out as particularly interesting are the oil, electric and natural gas supply industries and the metal industries, aluminium, nickel, copper, lead, zinc and iron ore extraction. Because of an abundance of water, hydro-electric power is cheap in Canada and this has greatly assisted the development of aluminium as a major industry. The leading banks are also an interesting medium of investment.

The procedures for buying Canadian shares are similar in principle to those for buying American shares. The investor may either acquire Canadian dollars much as he acquires American dollars and with these buy shares in Canada, or he may, if the shares have a market in London, buy them in London and avoid the trouble of having first to buy dollars.

The other Commonwealth country which has a share market of importance is Australia. Unlike Canada, it is a member of the Sterling Area. The Sterling Area consists of countries within and without (but they are mostly within) the Commonwealth, which acknowledge London as their financial centre, between which money including capital can move freely and whose currencies are fixed in relation to one another. They hold their foreign exchange reserves in London and mutually support one another in settling their payments with the rest of the world, particularly with the dollar countries.

Australia does not yet offer the investor quite as attractive opportunities as the United States or Canada but, like other countries in the Commonwealth, is reasonably well represented by companies registered in London or by companies whose shares are regularly dealt in on the London market.

The main sources of Australian income are wool, wheat and meat, which provide the bulk of the country's foreign income and form the basis of the country's economy. There is one important iron, coal and steel concern, an important group of lead and zinc producers, and there are one or two lesser gold mines; but otherwise the country unlike Canada is not rich in mineral wealth. Interests in these basic activities can be acquired by purchases of shares in London, e.g. the shares of pastoral companies, of trading concerns such as Dalgety & Co., of banks, of the steel company Broken Hill Proprietary, of the gold-mining companies and of the Broken Hill lead and zinc companies. If on the other hand the investor wants to take an interest in the country's growing manufacturing industries his purchases will have to be arranged through an Australian broker. His London broker will be able to do this for him; as he will also be able to provide him, through the same source, with information about the industries and companies in which he is contemplating making an investment.

For one reason or another there is not a great deal of British investors' interest in Australia outside the leading shares which can be bought in London. Part of the explanation for this lies in the comparative smallness in terms of population and remoteness of the country, part in the difficult labour relations which have existed in the past and part in the hazards of harvests and the sharp fluctuations which are apt to occur in wool and wheat prices over which the Australians have no control and which can have widespread and unpredictable effects on the economy. The population of the country is however rising and is bound to rise much more in the future; the country ought therefore to have a useful investment future.

No longer a member of the Commonwealth, South Africa is well represented in London in the fields of enterprise which are of major importance to the country—gold and diamonds, and particularly gold. Gold has an assured market and a fixed price. In this respect South Africa has a stable foundation for her economy subject to one condition, that the value of money remains stable and the things that South Africa has to import do not rise in price. This condition has not been met during the past twenty years and is not being met now. Because of the rising costs gold mining is becoming less profitable. South Africa would therefore like the price of gold to be raised. It can only be raised in any of the following conditions: if South Africa devalues the rand unilaterally; if the pound sterling is devalued; or if the American Government raises the dollar price of gold. South Africa and the United Kingdom will only devalue their currencies if for other reasons they should do so. They will not do so for the sake of making gold production more profitable or for the sake of increasing the value of their gold reserves. The American Government has even less reason to raise the price of gold. From its point of view, to raise the price of gold would be tantamount to devaluing the dollar, for which there is no need, and to making a gift to the gold-producing countries including Russia and to countries fortunate to possess already large gold reserves. The same results and, in American eyes, better results could be achieved by making loans or gifts to countries in cases of special need. The country in special need today may not be the country in special need tomorrow. The country in special need may also be in special need because it refuses to take the action necessary to stop inflation. Why therefore make indiscriminate grants, such as would be entailed in a general rise in the price of gold, when the effects of the grants may be to confer benefits where they are not needed, withhold them where they may be needed and make it easier for countries to inflate their currencies at a time when all constructive policy is aimed at eliminating inflation? The United States is not herself a large producer of gold, so that she has no direct interest in the matter.

Another argument has been advanced for raising the price of gold. If there should ever again be a world slump then raising the price of gold would be a quick and costless way of creating new demand. It is difficult to pronounce on the merits of this proposition in advance of the conditions which would make it a serious matter for consideration. Raising the price of gold would certainly increase the purchasing power of the gold-producing countries. It might also, for a time, save countries which were running into exchange difficulties from the necessity of cutting their imports. From that standpoint it would be a device meriting some consideration. But there would be alternatives. The country with exchange surpluses, particularly if it were the United States, could re-inflate demand by making loans on easy terms to the needy countries —it could reduce taxes at home, and increase personal spending power and it could ease the supply of money and cheapen it. To such measures there could be no objection. They would give help where it was needed, when it was needed and in the amounts that were needed and they would benefit and be seen to benefit the givers as well as the receivers.

How the argument will finally be decided only time will tell. There are signs that nations are at last beginning to look upon exchange and balance of payment problems as joint problems of the debtor and creditor—of the creditor to be a better customer and of the debtor to be a better supplier. This is how the matter should be viewed and must be viewed if the capitalist countries are to avoid weakening one another in unnecessary and wasteful economic rivalry. A rise in the price of gold would not hasten this development but would instead have the effect of obscuring very temporarily economic maladjustments between nations without providing a permanent solution and perhaps even at the cost of a valuable loss of time in finding one. In this as in other matters we come back to the basic problems of inflation and deflation of which exchange problems are merely one aspect.

Meanwhile, with the risk of inflation still present, gold shares remain, in principle, an unattractive medium of investment. With the price of gold fixed and costs more likely to rise than to fall, profits are liable to be adversely affected.

Apart from gold and diamond shares and some coal shares, South Africa is not an interesting field of investment. The country is not rich in other resources and there is always the risk of serious racial problems in the years to come.

So far as investments in the other Commonwealth countries are concerned the most noteworthy are Rhodesian copper, Indian oil and tea and Malayan tin and rubber. Of these the only one of serious interest to the British investor is Rhodesian copper. The Rhodesian copper producers are amongst the cheapest and most efficient in the world. While they face political problems, akin to those now existing in South Africa, the risk is not a new one and has not prevented the investor from reaping rich rewards. The long-term outlook for India, with its abnormally low living standards and its heavy over-population, is unpredictable, while Malaya is too unsettled politically to be of much interest to the investor. The high yields which have for long been available on tin and rubber shares go some way however to compensate for this.

CHAPTER X

INVESTMENT TRUST COMPANIES AND UNIT TRUSTS

General

Investment Trusts so called are broadly of two kinds: the Limited Liability Investment Company—in this country the commonest and the oldest, whose business it is to own and manage investments for their shareholders—and the Unit Trust. The former, being Companies and not Trusts, have an existence separate from their shareholders; the latter, being Trusts, are a form of mutual ownership from which the co-owners are free to withdraw at any time by demanding from the Trust a payment proportionate to their share of the value of the investments of the Trust. The holder of shares in an Investment Trust company (hereinafter referred to as Investment Companies) cannot realize his share of the investments of the company. If he wants to realize his investment he must go through the same procedure as he would in realizing his investment in any other company. He must find someone who is prepared to buy from him the shares he holds. This he may be able to do without much difficulty, if the shares are of one of the larger companies, by asking his broker to sell them. More often, he will have to wait a little, because most of the companies by public company standards are small and investors' interest in the shares is accordingly limited. But whether he has to wait or not he will in the normal course of events get a fair market price, based on what investors think of the company as a company and not on the value of the investments it holds, as in the case of a Unit Trust. If he wants to buy the shares, he may likewise be faced with delays.

Because the shareholder cannot withdraw the value of his proportionate interest in the investments of the company directly from the company, Investment Companies have been described as closed ended trusts as opposed to Unit Trusts which are open ended. The holders of shares or units, as they are more often called, in a Trust cannot of course withdraw precisely the sums they originally invested. The value of the units moves upwards and downwards with the value of the investments which the Trust holds and it is this value only which the holders can recover. It could not be otherwise, as one of the main objects of Unit Trust investment is to buy a spread of marketable investments whose values change from day to day.

Investment Companies

The earliest of these in their present form were formed in Scotland in the 1870's. The main object in forming them was to place at the disposal of investors the skill and investment knowledge of the founders. Those were days when investment carried many hazards that are non-existent today, when capitalism and joint stock finance were growing up, when there was much money to be made and to be lost in this country and in other countries whose resources this country as financial centre of the world had become interested in developing. Money was needed for growing industries and money could be lost in these industries. Investment skill was therefore essential in choosing investments. The early Investment Companies helped to provide this skill, as they also helped to raise the capital for capitalism's growing needs.

For the ordinary prudent man of those days the Funds, as Government securities were called, were the ideal form of investment: the Government paid its debts—money kept its value. He could not grow rich by investing in the Funds; but if he had grown rich he could be sure of keeping what he had, by doing so. Yet there was money to be made if he was not in industry and had money to invest in industry or in the other new services which were being developed. There was also money to be lost. He might pick an investment with care and yet find he had picked the wrong one, perhaps because he had been unlucky and perhaps because he had been defrauded. Investment companies helped to solve this problem by providing skill and investment spread. The investor in them did not have to decide for himself in which particular cotton mills, railways, banks or engineering concerns he was to invest his savings. Investment Companies decided that for him. The arrangement was convenient and the practice of forming Investment Companies grew, spreading in time as it was bound to do to London, where Robert Fleming of Dundee, one of the pioneers, in due course established himself, and to other parts of the world.

As might be expected, Investment Companies have over the years had their ups and their downs, with the trade cycle the main influence on their short-term fortunes. The late twenties were years of rising stock market prices when a good deal of money was to be made by the investor who knew what to buy. They were therefore years particularly favourable to the formation of new companies.

The investor with £100 to invest might hope to increase his income by buying a spread of Ordinary shares while the dividends from Ordinary shares were rising. If at the same time he could borrow £100 and add this to the £100 he already had, he could buy £200 worth of Ordinary shares. Then if Ordinary dividends rose by say 20% the increase in the income from his net investment would be not 20% but at least 40%, if the Ordinary shares were already paying sufficient in dividends to meet the cost of interest on the borrowed £100. This as we noted in Chapter VII is what is called gearing and it is a way of investment open to the private investor and widely practised by Investment Companies to which it is well suited. The Investment Companies formed in the nineteen-twenties made a feature of gearing. When formed they would issue Debenture, Preference and Ordinary share capital in approximately equal amounts. For example a company might be formed with a total capital of £1,000,000, consisting of £300,000 of 4½% Debentures issued at par, £300,000 of 5% Cumulative Preference shares also issued at par and £400,000 of Ordinary stock. The total funds, i.e. £1,000,000, might be invested in Ordinary shares giving an average return of 6%. At the end of the first year a position on something like the following lines might emerge (see table on page 104).

The following year owing to dividend increases gross earnings might rise by £10,000 or by 16·7% to £70,000, not an unreasonable rise during a period of reviving trade. Then the earnings available for Ordinary dividends would rise from £27,500 to £37,500 or by 36·4% to the equivalent of 9·4% on

Dividends gross		£60,000
Expenses of Management		4,000
		56,000
Debenture Interest	£13,500	
Preference Dividends	15,000	28,500
Earnings available for Ordinary Stock		£27,500
Equivalent on Issued Capital to		6·875%
Dividend recommended		6·5%

the issued Ordinary capital (a 16·7% rise in total earnings would have produced a 36·4% rise in earnings for the Ordinary stock. The gearing would have been 36·4 ÷ 16·7 or 2·2). The company might not wish in such circumstances to raise its dividend by the full amount of the increase in earnings but might recommend a dividend of 8%.

Now, if 6% was the rate of dividend which investors had in mind when they originally subscribed for the company's Ordinary share capital and if nothing in the meanwhile had happened to make investors feel that a yield different from 6% was the right yield to expect on a stock of this class, then the Ordinary stock might now be valued at 26s. 9d. per £1 unit, at which price it would yield 6% on an 8% dividend. In practice, however, the price might be nearer to 30s. to yield slightly over 5%, for investors in the opportunistic mood of that time would already be looking forward to the next year with the possibility of a further increase in the Ordinary dividend.

The Ordinary dividend would also be looking safer as the following figures illustrate:

	Share of Profits or priority percentages)	
	end of first year %	end of second year %
Debenture Interest requirements	0– 24·1	0– 20·5
Preference Dividend ,,	24·1– 50·9	20·5– 43·2
Ordinary Dividend ,,	50·9– 97·3	43·2– 91·7
Reserves	97·3–100·0	91·7–100·0

The trouble was that gearing made Ordinary shares look very attractive while the profits and dividends of companies were rising. When they stopped rising and began to fall as they did from about 1930 onwards a very different prospect faced the Ordinary shareholders of geared and especially of highly geared Investment Companies. And there was much disappointment amongst the investors as the result, a disappointment from which they have not yet fully recovered. In spite of very good performances during the post-war years of inflation and steadily rising dividends, Investment Company managements have never reacquired the prestige of their earlier, formative years. Gearing has been revealed as a trick which works very well if the managers of an investment fund know when to sell or if dividends continue to rise, but it does not work permanently to the advantage of the investor and can work very much against him.

The failure of the Investment Companies to regain their former status is best revealed by the tendency for the prices of the majority of shares to sell in the market below the values they would realize if the companies were wound up and the surplus assets, after paying off the outstanding Debenture and Preference stocks in full, were distributed amongst the Ordinary shareholders. It would be difficult to start a new Investment Company today without the Ordinary shares instantly falling to a discount below their issued prices, a circumstance which suggests that investors place a lower value on the skill of Investment Company managers than the remunerations they draw for their services. In the light of the performance of most Investment Companies in the admittedly favourable conditions of recent years, this is a judgment that is difficult to justify.

Investment Companies are taxed on the same principles as other companies except that most of their income has already been taxed at source. They can claim exemption from corporation tax on income from companies which has already borne corporation tax but they must pay corporation tax on foreign income and on interest income, including Government interest, which has not borne the tax. Against this income, they can charge their own Debenture interest if any. In regard to foreign income and in regard to interest income, Investment Companies are therefore in an inferior position to private investors who are not liable to pay corporation tax.

Unit Trusts

Unit Trusts are of more recent origin than Investment Companies, the first of the British ones dating back only to 1931. Apart from the important distinction between them and Investment Companies, to which reference has already been made, there are two other main distinctions. They have as a general rule no gearing. The investor in the Unit Trust is making a straightforward purchase of a spread of shares which, after allowing for expenses, have exactly the value of the money he is investing. And they are Trusts. A Trust Deed lays down how each Trust is to be run. A Trustee, usually the Trustee Department or Trustee Company of one of the large banks, holds the investments on behalf of the Unit holders, while a separate company, whose powers, obligations and basis of remuneration are defined in the Trust Deed, manages the investments. The basis of remuneration varies from Trust to Trust, but in the case of one of the large Trusts, it consists of a Preliminary charge, not exceeding 2%, which is included in the issue price of each unit and an annual charge, not exceeding $\frac{3}{8}$ of 1% of the capital value of the Trust, which is taken out of the net revenue.

The earliest Unit Trusts were Fixed Trusts. That is to say the portfolios of the Trusts were made up of a number of identical units of investment fixed in composition; the total value of a unit of investment might change but it continued to consist of the same specified and well-spread securities. Thus the investor always knew in just what underlying securities he was acquiring an interest. There were no problems of management, these having been decided when the Trusts were set up and the portfolio was settled. The disadvantages of this method of investment, however, soon became apparent. Complete fixity involved the continued purchase of shares which, as conditions changed, the prudent investor would not wish to continue buying and neglected investments whose merits were not so easy to see or did not exist at the time when the Trusts were formed. Moreover, as the prices of the individual securities making up the unit changed, one or two shares could come to have an excessive importance in the portfolio. As these disadvantages became apparent fixity gave way to flexibility

INVESTMENT TRUST COMPANIES

and the new Trusts formed all gave discretion to the managers to vary their investment portfolios and the proportions in which individual shares were held.

Unit Trusts whether of the fixed or flexible variety have usually confined their investments to Ordinary shares and over the years since they were formed this policy has paid very well. One important Trust group has been able to show that an investment in its Trusts which gave an income of $4\frac{1}{2}\%$ on the money invested in 1932 was giving an income of $14\frac{3}{8}\%$ on the original money by 1956. This contrasted with the steady $4\frac{3}{8}\%$ that would have been obtained on a gilt-edged investment over the same period. As there was a considerable fall in the value of money over this period, the gilt-edged investor suffered a reduction in his real income from $4\frac{3}{8}\%$ to $1\frac{5}{8}\%$ whereas the Unit Trust investor actually gained, his real income yield rising from $4\frac{1}{2}\%$ to $5\frac{3}{8}\%$. This satisfactory result was achieved from a list of investments, recognized to be in the highest class, the aggregate annual dividends from which, as received by the Trust, fell on only 7 out of the 25 occasions; and then mainly during the early years, when exceptional conditions prevailed throughout industry.

From the income point of view the investor who spreads his risks will also have very much less to fear than the investor who selects for example one share and invests all his money in it. A good spread of investments averages the losses as well as the gains of the investments chosen. Had for example the investor of 1932 confined his interest to one particular Ordinary share, Harrods, a well-known and highly regarded one which was included in the portfolio of the above Trust, he would have held his income position more or less steady until the war years and then as the result of war-time shortages have suffered a very sharp reduction. Recovery would have been rapid immediately after the war but thereafter progress would have been slow. It is for this reason a great mistake for investors to judge the virtues of investing in Ordinary shares by the experience of one. It is the group that matters and the group that makes them sounder than other classes of investment.

The soundness of an investment in a good spread of Ordinary shares is in fact well attested by the experience of time. Any investor in 1900, 1910, 1920, 1930, 1940 or in 1950 or in any of the intervening years who had bought a balanced spread of the leading industrial shares of the time, would be very much better off today than if as an alternative he had invested his money in Fixed Interest securities of the very highest class. There would have been years, the depressed years after the first war and after the economic collapse in 1929–31, when he would have had very serious anxieties about his position, but his anxieties would have passed. In the long run his position would have come right provided he had kept his head, and not been panicked into selling at a depressed level.

Yet the sharp fluctuations which can occur in the prices of Ordinary shares and through them in the prices of the units of Unit Trusts do raise problems for the investor for which there is no entirely satisfactory answer. One of the Trusts to which we have been referring made its first issue of sub-units in 1931 at a price of 31s. 9d. The price fell later that year to 25s. 6d. Thereafter it rose and fell until a high point of 53s. 3d. was reached in 1937. Then the threat of a renewed world economic depression followed later by war lowered the prices of Ordinary shares until by 1940 the price of the units was down to 21s. 7½d. From then onwards the price recovered rapidly and by the end of the war had regained all its losses since 1937. For the next few years the price continued to fluctuate upwards and downwards, rising to 65s. 9d. in 1947, falling to 46s. 5¼d. in 1949 and rising again to 58s. 6d. in 1951 when the Trust, which was a fixed one, was terminated and merged into a flexible one.

Investors experienced enough to ignore such fluctuations and well enough off financially not to have to worry about them, would have come out well in the end. But at the time, when their investments were showing heavy losses on their purchase prices, they could not have known what the end would be. Nor, in the nature of things, can the investor ever know what the end will be. He may look backwards and see that Ordinary shares have proved sound investments. He cannot look forward and know that they will prove sound investments. The Unit Trust, one way or another based on a spread of Ordinary shares, cannot for this reason answer all the requirements of the investor. It cannot guarantee the same income from year to year and it cannot offer protection against the possibility of an immediate fall in the value of the investor's capital. It can however offer the small investor a readily available and inexpensive means of buying Ordinary shares which, because of the multiplicity of small holdings he would require to have, to obtain a proper spread, would otherwise lie beyond his reach, and it can, in doing so, offer him an investment which over the years has, as we saw, more than fully offset the effects of inflation in terms of both income and capital.

After remaining dormant for many years, the Unit Trust movement came actively to life towards the end of 1958 with the formation of several new Trusts. These Trusts provided no services that were not already being offered by existing Trusts. The development was none the less useful in highlighting the advantages of this particular mode of investment. It is desirable however that the publicity attaching thereto should not obscure, in the minds of the small investor, the hazards inseparable from all purchases of Ordinary shares.

The investor with large sums of money to invest is in a position to establish a well-balanced Ordinary share portfolio of his own. Provided he can secure good advice in the selection of individual Ordinary shares, he therefore stands in no special need of the services provided by either the Investment Company or the Unit Trust unless he is interested in them as individual investments in their own rights. The special need which the Investment Company and the Unit Trust meets is the investment need of the small investor who does not have sufficient funds to establish a balanced Ordinary share Fund and who also lacks the skill to make selections on his own account. There is the convenience too, which applies equally to the large investor, that the investor receives a single dividend regularly every half year together in the case of the Unit Trust with a short report and audited account, telling him how his investment has fared, in place of the many smaller payments and other communications he would receive, if he held the same spread of investments directly himself. Of the two the Unit Trust meets his need best, not only because of the more speculative nature of the Ordinary shares of Investment Companies resulting from gearing but also because he can realize his investment at any time by going direct to the

Unit Trust instead of having to find a buyer in the market. This latter advantage may be small in normal times but in time of difficulty, when it is most likely to be put to the test by investors wishing to realize their investments, it may be considerable. The liquidity of the Unit Trust depends not merely on the public's interest in the particular Trust but in the public's interest in all the securities in which the Trust has, at the time, its funds invested. To realize the sums invested in the Trust by Peter Jones or James Smith, the Trust need only sell a portion of one of the many large and marketable securities in which its funds are invested. Alternatively, depending on market conditions, it can spread its sales over the whole range of securities in which it is interested.

PART III INVESTMENT POLICY

CHAPTER XI

THE NEED FOR AN ACTIVE INVESTMENT POLICY

The Importance of Good Timing

It has been proved, time and again, that it is not sufficient for the investor merely to buy the right securities. He must also buy them at the right time. The truth of this can be illustrated from the behaviour of *The Financial Times* index of Ordinary share prices over the eleven-year period 1947 to 1958. This index is compiled from the prices of 30 leading British Ordinary shares and shows how these prices compare each day with the prices of the same shares or their equivalents on 1 July 1935. That is to say, the index, when it is standing at 150, is reflecting a 50% rise in the prices of these Ordinary shares over their prices on 1 July 1935, or if it is standing at 175, a 75% rise in prices.

With this in mind, the figures on page 112 will be of interest. They show the high and low points recorded by the index at various times during the eleven-year period ending with the low point reached in the bear market of 1957–8, the average rate of dividend that was being paid on the shares which make up the index, and the average yield on the shares. For example, the index on 25 February 1958 stood at 154·4, say £154 8s. 0d. The rate of dividend paid on the index was 11·01% say £11 0s. 3d. The yield was therefore $\frac{11 \cdot 01}{154 \cdot 4} \times 100 = 7 \cdot 13\%$ or £7 2s. 6d.%.

The high point of the market over this period was reached on 21 July 1955 when the index touched 223·9. The subsequent low point was reached on 25 February 1958 when the index fell to 154·4. That means that an investor who had bought a spread of the 30 leading Ordinary shares which make up this index, on 21 July 1955, would have lost over 30% of his

			Price Index	Rate of Dividend %	Yield %
1947	17th January	.	140·6	4·72	3·36
,,	3rd September	.	104·2	5·32	5·11
1948	1st January	.	129·0	5·30	4·11
49	10th November	.	99·8	5·53	5·54
51	13th June	.	140·4	6·28	4·47
52	24th June	.	103·1	6·74	6·54
55	21st July	.	223·9	9·58	4·28
56	29th November	.	161·5	10·71	6·63
57	9th July	.	207·6	11·04	5·32
58	25th February	.	154·4	11·01	7·13

capital by the 25th February 1958; or to be more exact $\frac{223·9 - 154·4}{223·9} \times 100 = \frac{69·5}{223·9} \times 100 = 31\%$. He would subsequently have regained this loss if he had not lost heart and sold some or all of his shares; but the fact remains that at that time, if he had valued his investments, 31% would have been the scale of his losses, £30,000 if he had invested £100,000 and £3,000 if he had invested £10,000. Yet this loss would have had little connection with the circumstances of the individual companies in which he had invested his money; for during the period the average dividends on his investments rose from 9·58% to 11·01% and were still rising.

In fact, throughout the period 1947 to 1958, dividends were rising steadily from a rate of 4·72% on the index in 1947 to a rate of 11·01% in 1958. In spite of this, the investor buying at the wrong time, could have incurred heavy losses in 1947, again in 1949 when the index fell below its 1935 level, in 1952, in 1956 and in 1958. If he was a steady investor throughout the period, he could have afforded to ignore most of these losses for they were soon recovered; but if he was a spasmodic investor, attracted to Ordinary shares only because they were rising in price, he might have ended a very disillusioned and disappointed man.

The astute and speculative investor might on the other hand have found great opportunities in these sharp price movements for increasing his capital. To have done so he would have needed little knowledge of the circumstances of the individual companies, but a considerable amount of insight into the economic conditions of the time and of the action the Govern-

NEED FOR AN ACTIVE INVESTMENT POLICY 113

ment was likely to take to cope with the problems these conditions created. We shall say more about that later but let us consider now what investment action he might himself have taken.

Let us suppose that he started in January 1947 with a fund valued at £13,500, invested in the Ordinary shares which make up *The Financial Times* Ordinary share index. Let us suppose also that he gauged accurately the main movements in Ordinary share prices during the following eleven years, that he sold all his Ordinary shares close to the high points and that he reinvested the entire proceeds close to the succeeding low points. Finally let us suppose for the sake of arithmetical convenience, that his investment took the form of a Trust, which we shall call *The Financial Times* Index Trust, and that starting with a holding of 10,000 shares worth £13,500 he sold and bought his shares at the following prices:

1947 January	Sold at	£1·35 per share or 27s.
49 November	Bought at	£1·05 ,, ,, ,, 21s.
51 June	Sold at	£1·35 ,, ,, ,, 27s.
52 June	Bought at	£1·10 ,, ,, ,, 22s.
55 July	Sold at	£2·20 ,, ,, ,, 44s.
56 December	Bought at	£1·65 ,, ,, ,, 33s.
57 July	Sold at	£2·00 ,, ,, ,, 40s.
58 February	Bought at	£1·60 ,, ,, ,, 32s.

Had he been able to foresee events accurately, these are prices, in the circumstances visualized, at which he could easily have dealt. Having sold his 10,000 shares in January 1947 for 27s. he would have been able, with the resulting proceeds of £13,500, to buy in November 1949, 12,857 shares at 21s. per share. These he would in due course have sold at 27s. per share to realize £17,357. So with each upward movement of the market, he would have been able to increase the amount of cash he held, and with each downward movement of the market, the number of shares he held, until when he sold in July 1957, he would have had a cash holding of £42,078. This he would have invested in shares at 32s. per share, in February 1958, to give him a total holding of 26,299 shares compared with his original holding of 10,000 shares. Subsequently *The Financial Times* index rose to over 220 (or say 44s. per share), giving the total investment holding a value of over £55,000 or more than four times its 1947 value.

His capital and income position in February 1958 would as the result compare as follows with the capital and income position of the inactive investor who, having bought his 10,000 units in 1947, took no further action throughout the period.

	Active Investor Capital	Income	Inactive Investor Capital	Income
1947 January	10,000 shares	£472	10,000 shares	£472
1958 February	26,299 ,,	£2,895	10,000 ,,	£1,101
% increase	163%	513%	nil	133%

For the purpose of calculating income it is necessary to assume that each share has a nominal value which in this case we have taken to be 20s. Although as we said elsewhere, nominal values for shares are both unnecessary and undesirable, the assumption is unavoidable in this case because the dividends are expressed as percentages. 10,000 shares then have a nominal value of £10,000. The rate of dividend on *The Financial Times* index in January 1947 was 4·72% (see page 112). Therefore the income was £472. The income in 1958 was similarly calculated by using the dividend rates then appropriate.

To return to the main question, it is not suggested that such a gain in capital and income from following an active investment policy, is either a reasonable expectation or an attainable one. It is neither, but it is suggested, that to focus attention on the qualities of individual investments without regard to the climate of investment at the time, is to lose sight of an important investment consideration. By buying Ordinary shares at the wrong time, the investor would have lost some of his capital for a time, even although his income continued to rise. By buying them at the right time and selling them at the right time, he could have added greatly to his capital and income. It was not, in other words, sufficient for him to know that companies would be making larger profits and would be paying larger dividends on their Ordinary shares. He also, as we shall see, had to know that there would be a sharp rise in interest rates (Ordinary shares were yielding more than twice as much in February 1958 as they were yielding in January 1947) and that it would occur in spasms and not steadily throughout the period.

The Rate of Interest and Security Prices

We have already said a good deal about the rate of interest and emphasized its importance from the point of view of the control of the economy and we shall have more to say later when we discuss the considerations which have to be taken into account in trying to form a view about its future course. For the present we will be concerned only to show how and why the rate of interest affected the prices of Ordinary shares during the period under review. The following table taken in conjunction with that on page 112 helps to do this.

		Ordinary Share Yield %	Yield on 2½% Consols %	Price of Consols
1947	January 17	3·36	2·54	98½
	September 3	5·11	2·95	84¾
48	January 1	4·11	3·06	81¾
49	November 10	5·54	3·77	66¼
51	June 13	4·47	3·83	65¼
52	June 24	6·54	4·52	55¼
55	July 21	4·28	4·23	59
56	November 29	6·63	4·98	50¼
57	July 9	5·32	5·06	49½
58	February 25	7·13	5·17	48¼

Between January 1947 and February 1958 the yield on 2½% Consols doubled. Between January 1947 and February 1958 the yield on Ordinary shares also approximately doubled. As the period advanced, investors expected a higher rate of interest on the money they invested. On the other hand, the prices of Ordinary shares, taking the period as a whole, rose and they rose because the rise in dividends slightly more than compensated for the rise in interest rates. The Ordinary dividend paid when the yield was 3·36% in January 1947 was 4·72%, whereas when the yield was 7·13% in February 1958 the Ordinary dividend paid was 11·01% or well over double the 1947 amount.

The table also shows that the yield on Ordinary shares was at all times higher than the yield on 2½% Consols, usually about one-third to one-half higher. The reason for this was that the income from 2½% Consols was considered to be safer than the income from Ordinary shares. There were two occasions however when this was not so, on 21 July 1955 when the two yields were practically identical and on 9 July 1957 when they were again close together but not quite so close. These were also the occasions when Ordinary shares reached their peak prices. Investors had in fact begun to think that Ordinary shares were becoming too dear in relation to the safest Fixed Interest securities and were beginning to sell them; or viewed in another way, the rate of interest relating to Ordinary shares had become too low.

Why was the rate of interest rising throughout the period? There was one simple reason—inflation. The purchasing power of the pound was falling more rapidly than the purchasing power of other currencies and this was causing periodical balance of payments crises which called for immediate attention. The Socialists while they were in power tried to check inflation by a variety of controls on the demand for goods and by maintaining a very substantial Budget surplus, trying the while to keep interest rates artificially low. But because they failed to establish confidence in their ability to succeed, their efforts were not successful either in checking inflation or in keeping interest rates low, as the rise in the yield on $2\frac{1}{2}$% Consols from 2·54% in January 1947 to 3·83% in June 1951 showed. The Conservatives when they came to power towards the end of 1951 adopted a different policy. They abandoned their predecessor's policy of artificially cheap money and increased the short-term rate of interest, first by modestly raising the Bank Rate from 2% to $2\frac{1}{2}$% in November 1951 and later in the following March more sharply from $2\frac{1}{2}$% to 4%. By these measures, which reduced the demand for money, and by keeping a tight control over the supply of money, they achieved for a time a considerable amount of success—certainly much more than the Socialists had achieved in their time. Unfortunately by the Autumn of 1953 they began to get worried about the dangers of a trade recession. They reduced the Bank Rate to $3\frac{1}{2}$% and again in the following May to 3%. The action was premature. The cost of living which had not yet stopped rising but which had been fairly stable during 1953 and 1954 began to move up again. The inflow of gold reflecting the improved position of sterling, which had been substantial during 1953 and the first six months of 1954, went into reverse and the Government was forced again to take action, by raising the Bank Rate, first to $3\frac{1}{2}\%$ in January 1955 and then to $4\frac{1}{2}\%$ in February 1955. Finally in September 1957 it was raised to 7%.

Viewing the period as a whole the one continuous feature was the presence of inflation. It had at no time been effectively eliminated. There was therefore no basis for confidence so far as the rate of interest was concerned. With this in mind the investor should have been biased in favour of Ordinary shares but watchful of the effect of the rate of interest on their prices. Of any untoward rise in Ordinary share prices and fall in Ordinary share yields, such as that which occured in 1955 and again in 1957 which overlooked the renewed weakness of sterling and therefore the probability of a further rise in the rate of interest, he should have been suspicious. He ought on no account to have invested his money in undated or long-dated Fixed Interest securities, as their prices were certain to be exposed to the full effects of the rise in interest rates, without the offsetting compensation of a rise in interest income. He might on the other hand have invested in Fixed Interest securities with early dates of redemption. The ideal short-dated security would have been the Treasury Bill but only slightly inferior would have been securities redeemable within one or two years. By investing in either of these, the investor would have been able to preserve his capital and in due course reap the advantage of the higher level of interest rates.

Ordinary Dividend Income

The period under review was one when Ordinary dividend income presented very few problems. Trade was good. Profits and Ordinary dividends were rising. It might not have been so, had more success attended the Government's efforts to check inflation, for then, as the anti-inflation measures took effect, profits which are the margin between prices and costs would have been narrowed by the upward pressure of wages and the halting of price increases. Wages would have stabilized themselves in time as rising unemployment restored competition to the labour market, but the first effects of competition would have been felt by prices and profits. It might also not have been so had inflation been a purely British malady. Then in order to keep our prices competitive with the rest of the world, more drastic measures might have been required.

Ordinary dividend income cannot therefore be taken for granted any more than the rate of interest. Both have to be weighed carefully in the balance by the investor. On the other hand with modern techniques for promoting employment, Ordinary dividend income is likely to be better looked after in the future than it was in the past. We have indeed seen that during the ten years to 1958, whenever trade was threatened even on a modest scale, action was quickly, and indeed too soon, taken to ease the situation. The battle in the future may therefore continue to be against inflation rather than against depression; and in that event of the two variables in valuing securities, the more difficult to assess may be the rate of interest.

Forecasting the Rate of Interest

Inflation has a natural tendency to force up the rate of interest but different Governments are likely to tackle the problem of inflation differently and indeed the same Government may be compelled by the force of public opinion to approach it differently at different times. The investor must therefore remain alert at all times to the likely nature of Government policy. As experience has so far revealed itself in this matter, Labour Governments have favoured high taxation as the principal antidote to inflation while Conservative Governments have favoured high short-term interest rates and, where possible, economy. Neither has shown a readiness to tackle the root cause, which lies in the high level of its own expenditures.

As to the evidences of inflation there are many—some to which the Government of the day attaches more importance than to others. The cost of living is probably the most representative single one and the one which affects electors most directly. Yet the cost of living has hitherto had much less influence on Government activities than the country's external balance of payments and in particular whether the country was gaining gold or losing gold. This is paradoxical in a way, for the real evil is that the cost of living is rising. When the cost of living is rising and when therefore money is

NEED FOR AN ACTIVE INVESTMENT POLICY

falling in value, there is no basis for confidence in money, either at home or abroad. People at home want to convert their money, as soon as possible, into goods a proportion of which will be imported goods, and people abroad want to withdraw, with the least delay, any money they have here, lest it depreciate further in value. Hence the pressure on sterling and hence the loss of gold, for gold is the currency with which countries pay their debts, one to another.

The trend of the cost of living is then the most important single index of inflation, but the balance of payments, reflected in the sterling dollar exchange rate and in the monthly trade figures of imports and exports, may immediately have more effect on the Government. Both of these should be watched by the investor therefore, although they suffer the disadvantage that they relate to what has happened rather than to what is going to happen. So far as what is going to happen is concerned, he can hope to do no more than form a view. In forming a view however there is a lot of information on which he can draw and which taken together can give him a pretty good idea of the drift of events. It includes wage rates and current wage awards, the employment and unemployment position and the relationship of the latter to the recorded number of unfilled jobs, Government current revenue and expenditures, present and planned Government capital expenditures, as well as many other indicators of the course of future economic development such as industrial building plans, machine tool new orders and new house building.

It is also important that the weekly return of the Bank of England be studied as one of the best guides to how the Government is facing up to the day to day problem of controlling the supply of money. This return in addition to giving useful information about the money in circulation (whether the amount of cash which the public is using is rising or falling) gives some indication of how tight or how easy the supply of money is being kept. In particular it shows the level of Bankers deposits, one of the two constituents, the other being cash, of the cash reserves of the Clearing Banks, the reserves (see Appendix V) on which they found their lending policies. Another useful return is the monthly return of the Clearing Banks, which shows, month by month, changes in the total cash reserves of the Clearing Banks, in the total sums of money held by the public on deposit with the Clearing Banks, in the total investments of the Clearing Banks and in the total loans to the public by the Clearing Banks.

The statistics which inform the investor on the threat of inflation will also inform him on the threat of deflation, the problem which in pre-war years was his greatest cause of anxiety. In the world of today deflation may seem a remote threat but the investor would be foolish for this reason to dismiss it from his mind. War and its aftermath have a great responsibility for the present economic state of the world. The leading nations although not at war are spending considerable sums of money annually in maintaining a state of preparedness for war. If this exceptional demand were removed, over-capacity in many directions would make its re-appearance and statesmen might for a time be sorely tried to find alternative ways of making use of it or to provide employment for the people released from the manufacture of arms. Even without this subtraction from demand the American economy has already found some difficulty in absorbing the immense output which its industries are capable of producing.

Conclusion

There would be less occasion for the investor to worry about these matters if once he purchased a security, he ceased to care about its price provided he obtained from it the income he expected when he made the purchase. In fact investors do care about what happens to the prices of securities they buy, for the reason that while they buy for income, they want, if they can, to increase their capital and do not like to see it being lost. An investor who buys a security at one price and finds that soon afterwards he could have bought it at a lower price without anything having happened, so far as he can discover, to affect the quality of the security, is bound to feel that he has bought unwisely or that he has been cheated and would be less than human if he did not want to know why. As we have attempted to show he has not been cheated but he has bought unwisely because he took insufficient account of the general economic situation at the time. In this he was not alone. Many other investors did the same. But there were also other investors who did not make his mistake. In future he must try to be one of these other investors.

The aim of this chapter has been to show how much money can be made by good buying and selling and to indicate some of the things that the investor must learn in order to achieve this. It is necessary to add however that there are times when markets appear to make nonsense of all attempts at rational appraisal and the investor is faced with the dementing question of deciding whether to throw caution overboard, attribute it to ignorance of new trends and new ideas which have rendered obsolete the old patterns of thought, and follow the market. He will be very foolish to do so. If he does he is quite likely to do so just when the tide is beginning to turn in favour of the stand he has taken. His right course of action in these times is to maintain a balanced portfolio by selling what looks very dear and buying what looks very cheap and placing a strong emphasis on yields and the preservation of his capital in money terms, in the knowledge that if the worst comes to the worst, he may be poorer than he might otherwise have been but will still have resources available to take advantage of opportunities when reason returns, which it always does. Prices of securities are made by opinion. Those who make opinion and lead opinion are in a much better position to "get in" and "get out" of over priced investments than the ordinary investor who has only his knowledge and common sense to guide him. To these qualities he should hold fast, respecting the reasons and questioning the emotions underlying current market trends, and refusing to go out of his depths until he knows he can swim. If he does not, he is not an investor.

CHAPTER XII

THE GENERAL INVESTMENT BACKGROUND

Inflation is antagonistic to the interests of the Investor

Investors old enough to remember the great Trade Depression of 1929–33, if faced with the choice of a return to economic conditions as they were then and the maintenance of economic conditions as they are now, might decide in favour of economic conditions as they are now. In the slump of 1929–33 countless millions were lost in Ordinary shares, Preference shares and even in what had previously been regarded as first-class industrial Debenture stocks. Today losses on industrial Ordinary shares, where they occur, often have much less to do with the circumstances of the individual company or with trade but owe themselves to conditions (including high interest rates) for which the Government of the day bears a considerable responsibility. Profits in the aggregate have been rising year in and year out since the end of the war and dividends have been rising with them.

Yet a reckoning based on these considerations alone would be a superficial one. Inflation hits the investor in three important ways.

(1) It undermines the standard—money—by which the value of investments is measured.

(2) Because it gives an appearance of undeserved gain to the investor in Ordinary shares, it attracts the attention of predatory Governments who like to think of the shareholders' function as parasitic.

(3) It forces a rise in interest rates which undermines the values of existing fixed income investments.

(1) While Ordinary shareholders have had some success in contracting out of the effects of the inflation which has occurred during the past twenty years, holders of Government securities have suffered a two-third reduction in the value of their income. It is not an excuse that investors in

Government securities were not compelled to buy them. They were sold by the Government under an assumed warranty that they were in all respects sound securities and were acquired by investors in the reasonable belief that they were what they purported to be. As the total outstanding amount of the Government Debt is in the region of £34,000 million and as the total of all kinds of Fixed Interest securities in which investors may invest greatly exceeds this total it can be readily appreciated how considerable has been the scale of the losses from this cause.

(2) Governments who debase currencies have a habit of regarding money appreciation, resulting from a rise in prices, as gain. The man who owned a house in 1935 priced at £1,000 is no richer today because by virtue of inflation the same house is now priced at £3,000. But some Governments do not regard this as so. By extending the tax on short-term gains to long-term gains in the 1965 Act, the British Government has brought within the range of taxation, all gains accruing and realized after 6th April 1965 on the disposal of assets, with certain specific exceptions such as the taxpayer's principal residence. If the result had been to tap a useful new source of revenue, the tax might have been justified. Its main effect in practice has however been to tax gains which are not true gains and to distort market prices by encouraging investors, in order to limit their tax liabilities, to sell stocks on which they are showing losses and which are already undervalued, with the object of establishing losses which they can set off against gains on high priced shares which they feel they can no longer postpone selling.

(3) Weak Governments battling against inflation and relying on a popular vote for their election are reluctant to take the measures which would root out inflation on a basis fair to all. They hesitate to tax because taxes are unpopular. They hesitate to cut their expenditures because expenditures are popular. So they resort to an expensive policy of inducements. Knowing that the solution lies in part in inceased saving, they endeavour to encourage new saving by increasing the rewards of new saving. They raise

interest rates. New saving is thereby made more attractive but the immediate effect, as we saw in the last chapter, is to depreciate the value of existing savings, expressed in terms of money roughly in proportion to the rise in interest rates. The effect of the rise in interest rates between 1951 and 1958 was to cut thousands of millions of pounds from the realizable value of all forms of existing savings. If in the result inflation had been averted investors might have had less reason to complain. In due course interest rates would have been reduced—the value of money would have been maintained and the value of past savings both in real and money terms would have been restored. What in fact did happen was that the existing stock of savings both in real and in monetary terms suffered severe and, measured in real terms, permanent depreciation. Ordinary shares because of rising dividends rose in money value but by an amount barely sufficient to offset the fall in the value of money.

Inflation in fact imposes severe penalties on the investor and investors who favour it as a continuing policy show a foolish disregard of their interests. They may, although this is now to be expensive, be able to profit from it by borrowing other people's savings on fixed capital terms (that is on terms that involve paying back no more than the money borrowed plus interest) and investing the proceeds in Real Property or in Ordinary shares. The gains they make in this way will not however be gains by investors as a whole, but deductions from the savings of the stable elements in Society who, in spite of discouragement, continue to place their faith in the value of money by lending to the Government and to other borrowers on fixed interest or fixed capital terms.

The penalties imposed on the investor by inflation may be best illustrated by using the figures from *The Financial Times* index given in the last chapter, pages 112 and 115. An investor in January 1947 concentrating on securities of the highest quality might have invested £50,000 in 2½% Consols and £50,000 in the thirty leading Ordinary shares which make up the index. If he had done so his capital and income position would have been as follows:

	Price 17/1/47	Yield %	Capital	Income
2½% Consols	98½	2·54	£50,000	1,270
Ordinary Shares	140·6	3·36	50,000	1,680
			£100,000	2,950

If in the meanwhile he had made no changes in his investments his position in February 1958 would have been:

	Price 25/2/58	Yield %	Capital	Income
2½% Consols	48¾	5·17	£24,500	1,270
Ordinary Shares	154·4	7·13	55,000	3,920
			£79,500	5,190

January 1947 was a high point in the Ordinary share market and February 1958 a low point, so that the comparison does less than justice, from the capital point of view, to the fortunes of Ordinary shareholders over the period. Even so the investor came badly through the experience in terms of capital. Between January 1947 and February 1958 the cost of living rose by approximately 70%. If therefore he was merely to preserve his capital his investments in February 1958 would have had to be worth £170,000 in total compared with the £79,500 which they were in fact worth. On the other hand he did not fare badly from the income point of view. Allowing for the rise in the cost of living he would have needed an income of £5,015 in 1958 to give him the same purchasing power as he had had in January 1947. Because of the rise in Ordinary dividends from 1951 onwards his income was slightly more than this. This was no more than his due however, considering that in the ten years before 1947 Ordinary shareholders had as a whole received no increase in their income in spite of a rise of nearly 100% in the cost of living.

The End of Inflation may be in Sight

Inflation is recognized by most people to be an evil. The only reason why it has continued during the post-war period has been the difficulty of reconciling its absence with the provision of adequate stimulants to employment and output. As each onslaught has been made upon inflation employment and output have fallen and the Government has been condemned for favouring policies of industrial stagnation and unemployment. The result has been a growing public insistence on a return to conditions as they were, an insistence which the Government has found itself unable to ignore. Yet the insistence has been based on fears for which there was no foundation. Because output is cut and unemployment rises, it does not follow that the process will continue, or that the Government will wish it to do so. The aim of Government policy in the circumstances is merely to create an environment in which automatic annual increases in wages and prices will not occur. When that is done and industry and labour come to recognize stable money as a goal in itself to be striven for, there will be no difficulty about ensuring and maintaining a sufficiency of demand to provide for the fullest employment of existing resources and a sound base for a steadily rising level of output.

The problem of inflation is in fact not insoluble, and indeed the efforts to find a solution may in due course be greatly reinforced by developments in the United States. Most of the great inflations in the past have arisen out of the demands of war and out of the economic disturbances set up by war. In the long run however the capitalist system has shown a greater propensity to produce than to consume. In the United States, in recent years, consumption has not kept pace with production, in spite of considerable increases in defence expenditures and of equally considerable increases in borrowings by consumers, against their future incomes, for the satisfaction of their needs in the present. Perhaps the American Government will increase its expenditure on defence without exacting an equal increase in taxes. Perhaps private citizens will continue to spend more and more of their future incomes to gratify their present wishes, but all history suggests that sooner or later there must be a reckoning. High Government expenditure when it leads to inflation, renders high taxation necessary as a corrective. People dislike high taxation and faced with the logic of the situation, demand Government economy. High private indebtedness creates private economic instability. While incomes remain secure and prices tomorrow seem likely to be higher than they are today, no one worries. But if for any reason incomes become insecure, perhaps because taxation has had to be increased sharply to curb inflation, or because Government expenditures have had to be reduced in order to avoid the necessity of a rise in taxation, the situation could turn round rapidly, especially if it were reinforced, as it might well be in these circumstances, by a tightening of the supply of money and a consequent rise in the cost of borrowing. Then people, instead of buying ahead of their incomes and thereby supplementing demand, might start to repay their debts. This, if it happened, would result in a serious loss of business and income to those who depend for their livelihoods on hire purchase and instalment buying and on other forms of buying such as house purchase, which has in recent years been financed extensively out of private borrowing.

Because of the economic importance of the United States any setback in that country would have repercussions all over the world. Commodity prices would fall. The purchasing power of the countries which gain their livelihood mainly from the production of foodstuffs and industrial raw materials would fall and that in turn would affect the export income of the industrial nations amongst which the United Kingdom and Germany rank as the most important, after the United States.

One other factor, affecting particularly the American economy, ought not to be ignored. This is the extent to which Common stock prices have been raised to levels which can only be justified on the assumption that there cannot be another slump and that inflation must remain as a permanent feature of economic life. In view of what has been said above it is difficult to find any sound basis for the conviction. It is true that retail prices have been rising. It is true also that profits and dividends have been rising but only moderately by comparison with profit and dividend expectations as reflected in current share prices and yields. Business has for the most part remained competitive, with profits liable to suffer sharp setbacks on fairly minor recessions. An important reinforcement of total demand in recent years has come from the war in Vietnam against which a reaction has now set in, calling for large reductions in expenditure. In this respect there is a similarity between the situation today and the situation when the last Republican administration took office at the height of the Korean war. In other respects the situation is less favourable. Common stock prices are very much higher in relation to earnings. The dollar is no longer unchallengeably the strongest currency in the world. It too has problems which the Government can no longer afford to ignore and is not ignoring. Money has become very tight and very dear, thus making available attractively high yielding Fixed Interest securities as alternatives to Common stocks, as doubts increase about the durability of inflation. There are in fact danger signals in plenty which it would be unwise to disregard.

The persistent debasement of currencies since the war has had the predictable effect of destroying confidence in nearly all money. The result is that no currency is completely secure. Vast sums of money now encircle the world accepting responsibility to no country and ready at a moment's notice to move from where they detect weakness to where they anticipate strength, aggravating as they move the weaknesses and sometimes causing them, from which they are escaping. The harm done to the conduct of ordinary business has been enormous, forcing the Central Banks of the leading countries, time and again, to come to the assistance of currencies put under pressure by these activities. This joint action by Central Banks, fully supported by their Governments, is one of the most hopeful and constructive developments of recent times, which followed up, as it is being, by internal Government action to restrain demand, offers the reasonable prospect of an early end to the malignancy. In that event Common stock prices which have come to reflect in large measure the lack of confidence in money will suffer a setback.

Prices which rise to levels which prove in the light of cold reality to be unjustified, are apt to fall. As Common stock prices rise they generate a feeling of economic wellbeing and encourage expansive ways of life which otherwise people would not feel able to afford. As they fall they have the opposite effect. Security prices which are unduly inflated have economic implications therefore which those with long memories are unlikely to have forgotten. The Wall Street crash which began in 1929 was not merely the warning signal of the impending economic collapse; it was also one of the principal causes.

Viewing the future strictly through the eyes of the present, it is possible to erect a convincing argument in favour of the likely continuance of inflation. Inflation, provided it can be restrained, is much to be preferred to widespread depression and massive unemployment. For this reason organized labour, with unhappy recollections of the inter-war years, has ranged itself unequivocally on the side of policies which assure a high demand for the products of their labour. Nor is industry any less insistent on the importance of keeping its factories employed making goods for consumers, which consumers, if they have the money, would like to buy. It is common sense and these are powerful forces, representing a majority of the electorate, whose wishes no Government can afford to ignore.

Yet there is more to be said. The alternatives may now appear to be restrained inflation, or sound money and serious unemployment. But in the long run it will be impossible to restrain inflation, for in the long run everyone will lose faith in money. Equally it will be impossible to sustain full employment, if the consequence of inflation is to cause people, as in the United States, to run more and more into debt and to build up personal economic positions which become more and more unsound, the longer the inflation lasts. Then the gentlest of tugs on the reins of credit may be sufficient to set in motion a process of liquidation, which, gentle at first, gathers momentum as it progresses and people lose their jobs making goods previously sold on credit. Americans have learned from hard experience in the 1929 Wall Street crash the dangers of too much stock market credit. But they appear not to have learned yet the dangers of too much consumers' credit.

Governments are bound in fact to wage war against inflation and to search constantly for new ways of combating it. They may not be wholly successful in their endeavours, as they may not, for the same reason, be wholly successful in their endeavours to achieve full employment (for the two are more closely bound up together than is commonly realized); but they will have to achieve at least sufficient success, to keep alive some respect for the value of money and in particular for their own credit-worthiness as borrowers. The worker, the industrialist and the investor will not be foolishly neglectful of their respective interests, if they do what they can within reason to keep alive this respect. For the problem is not wholly a problem for Governments. It is also a problem for Society.

CHAPTER XIII

THE NEED FOR INVESTMENT SPREAD

Should Fixed Interest Securities be included?

The answer to this question depends on what view one has formed about the likely future of the value of money. If money continues to fall in value at a rate not less than 3% per annum, as some of the advocates of creeping inflation have suggested it may with safety be allowed to do, then there is no place for any holding of Fixed Interest securities in a permanent list of investments, at least for a taxpayer paying the current standard rate of income tax, unless the income offered is very high and very secure. Certainly there would be no place in such circumstances for a holding of Government securities at the existing level of prices. A Government security for example giving a yield of 5% gross, would provide a net yield after tax of £3 1s. 3d. If the purchasing power of money was falling at the rate of 3% per annum, £100 invested in the security would have a value of only £97 after one year in terms of the first year's pounds, so that at the end of the year the investor would be very little better off in spite of the interest he had received, than he was at the beginning. The process would be continuing moreover. His capital loss in the second year would be smaller (the equivalent of 3% of £97), but his income would also be smaller in the same ratio. The £3 1s. 3d. he received during the second year would have 3% less purchasing power than the £3 1s. 3d. he received during the first year. So each year his gain would be slight. If the annual inflation was greater than 3% he would be worse off and he would be still worse off, if as a surtax payer he was liable to pay a higher rate of tax than the standard rate assumed above.

Moreover as we saw in the previous chapter the losses may not be confined to the fall in the value of money. In money terms alone the investor in Consols lost half of his capital in eleven years. This half was further increased to nearly 70% by the fall in the value of money. In terms of 1958 pounds he had invested £85,000 in Consols in 1947 to find the investment worth only £24,500 in 1958. Against this loss of £60,000 he had received gross interest payments over the period of £14,000 (say £8,000 net after tax, in pounds which admittedly over the period had a greater value than 1958 pounds); a poor result for the safety he had looked for in Government securities and a poor advertisement of one of the securities in which Trustees are encouraged to invest, often on behalf of needy people, the funds of Trusts under their care.

If the investor was not a taxpayer, he would fare less badly and if at the time he invested interest rates were high, he would fare much less badly. But in no circumstances would he fare so well as the investor in Ordinary shares, even if in place of Government securities he bought high yielding Fixed Interest securities. An extra risk to his capital would attach to the extra yield he was obtaining which might and might not turn out satisfactorily, and he would still be denying himself the main protection against inflation which can be obtained only from real assets and their earnings, and from Ordinary shares, which represent real assets.

But as we have seen there is no certainty about future inflation. Inflation has shown itself today to be fairly intractable. But so was deflation fairly intractable in an earlier stage of our development. We overcame it and we may in the future overcome inflation. Assuming however that we never quite overcome it—that we continue to battle against it but without complete success. What then? There is none the less a place for some holding of Fixed Interest securities. We have seen that one of the principal weapons which the Government employs to fight inflation is dear money. Dear money has the effect of depressing the prices of all securities including Ordinary shares but it depresses the prices of these securities most which are not redeemable at an early date. Ordinary shares are by their nature irredeemable securities. So are Preference shares. So are some Debenture stocks and some Government stocks. But there are some Debenture stocks and many Government stocks where the obligation to redeem arises soon. There is a place for such stocks in all actively managed investment funds at times when a rise in interest rates is threatened.

THE NEED FOR INVESTMENT SPREAD

There are periods when inflationary pressures are stronger than they are at other periods, assuming inflation to be a continuing condition. During these periods the wise investor knowing that sooner or later the Government will act, should be realizing some of his Ordinary share profits and building up a fund for future use when interest rates are raised and the prices of Ordinary shares fall. He can build up this fund best by acquiring readily marketable short-dated Government securities. He may incur losses when he comes to realize these but they will be very considerably less than the losses he will have incurred if he has continued to hold a full list of Ordinary shares and he will have kept his money fully invested earning interest.

Is there, quite apart from this case for short-dated Fixed Interest securities, a case for Fixed Interest securities in their own right? In the opinion of the writer there is. The investor must beware of allowing his judgment to be influenced too much by contemporary tendencies. We have had inflation for a long time but there have also in the past been long spells of deflation. For the fifty years immediately before the first world war, money retained its purchasing power. During most of the twenty years which preceded the second world war, money gained in purchasing power. What will happen in the future, no one can with confidence say, but we can say that war has had much to do in the past with inflation and that Governments now are deeply concerned with the problem of overcoming it. The investor should bear this in mind. He should also bear in mind that in the natural course of events, goods become cheaper to produce, as improved methods of production are developed. The motor car and wireless set fell sharply in price during the inter-war years, not because wages were falling or the quality of the product was deteriorating but because knowledge of how to manufacture them was increasing and competition ensured that the consumer got the advantage. History may not in this respect repeat itself, but at least there are powerful pressures, in growing technological knowledge, which will go some of the way and may go all of the way, towards ensuring that money will in the long run keep its value.

The investor is primarily concerned with getting a good and safe return on his money. Provided inflation is abolished, he can secure a good and safe return on his money by holding the best Fixed Interest securities. He may be venturesome and he may wish to increase his income, but he should not suppose that there is any easy way of doing this which is not accompanied by risks that he may reduce his income. Fixed Interest securities are intrinsically safer than Ordinary shares and the investor who is taking a long view and wants primarily to preserve his capital and income should give due weight to this consideration by holding up to 50% of his total fund in Fixed Interest form. If he is venturesome and his circumstances permit him to incur greater risks, he may reasonably content himself with a lower and possibly much lower proportion in Fixed Interest securities than this and conversely. Also if he is an active investor, as it is desirable in the view of the writer that he should be, he may vary this proportion upwards or downwards, upwards when he believes Ordinary shares are becoming too dear in relation to Fixed Interest securities and downwards when he believes the reverse to be true. But in general, he should never lose sight of the need to balance his investment portfolio against the risks that he cannot hope to foresee. In holding securities he is dealing all the time in uncertain futures, not in assured pasts; and a degree of humility in his powers of prediction is at all times wise, as it is also wise that he should endeavour as a general rule to get the best value for his money in terms of income and security of income.

There was a time when a 100% investment in Fixed Interest securities was considered the hallmark of sound investment. Indeed, under the Trustee Act of 1925, Trustees were obliged, unless specifically empowered to do otherwise, to invest funds under their control wholly in specified Fixed Interest securities or in Real Estate but not in Ordinary shares. So to narrow the investment powers of Trustees was quite unjustifiable, in the light of the damage which inflation had done to the income from Fixed Interest securities and in the light of the more favourable experience of Ordinary shares under these conditions; but to move from this to the opposite extreme of excluding Fixed Interest securities from a soundly based investment portfolio would have been equally unjustifiable.

Ordinary Shares must be included and they should be well spread

Under the Trustee Investments Act, 1961, Trustees have been given general powers to invest in Ordinary shares. In order to exercise these powers, they must divide funds in their care into two parts equal in value at the time of the division, to be called the narrower range part and the wider range part. Narrower range investments consist of high grade Fixed Interest securities and a number of investments such as National Savings Certificates which are fixed in terms of capital. Wider range investments consist of the registered Preference and Ordinary shares of companies of a certain standing, incorporated in the United Kingdom, the shares of Building Societies which have qualified for Trustee status and the units or shares of Unit Trusts.

Power is taken in the Act to vary upwards the wider range part of Trustee funds, but in deciding initially to adhere to the present ratio, a very fair balance has been struck in all the circumstances. Certainly the Act represents a valuable step in the right direction. The only regret is that it should have been so long delayed.

According to estimates prepared by the London & Cambridge Economic Service covering the period from 1867 to 1925 and by Moody's Services Limited (covering the period from 1925 onwards) British Ordinary shares have risen in price approximately 600%. During the period 1867-1900 when commodity prices were falling, Ordinary shares nearly doubled in value. Since the beginning of the century, the rise in Ordinary share prices has little more than kept pace with the rise in commodity prices. Historically, therefore, inflation has not been a favourable influence. Ordinary shares have been able to neutralize its adverse influences. They have also been able to demonstrate their immense superiority, under these conditions, over Fixed Interest securities; but they have not gained on balance as much as they might have gained had the economic climate been consistently favourable to inflation-free expansion.

While Ordinary shares have over the years risen in price they have from time to time suffered sharp falls which, while they lasted, severely tested the nerves of their stoutest supporters. There was a prolonged decline in the prices of Ordinary shares during the seventies and eighties of the last century. During this period the value of money was rising and the price of $2\frac{1}{2}\%$ Consols was rising also. The Ordinary share enthusiast of those days would have needed strong nerves and might have been forgiven had he abandoned his convictions and temporarily sought shelter in the security of the Funds. He was again in trouble during the first ten years of this century, when in spite of rising commodity prices he was unable to maintain the value of his investments. This time, however, he was sharing his troubles with the holders of Government securities and he was able to console himself with the knowledge that his investments had shown satisfactory appreciation during the nineties. From the beginning of the 1914–18 war onwards, Ordinary share prices have suffered three major setbacks and two minor ones and enjoyed five major recoveries, each recovery carrying prices substantially above the peak prices earlier established. The setbacks have had a maximum duration of two or three years while the recoveries have been of a longer duration—from four to eight years.

If over a period of nearly 100 years when industry has had to contend with many different kinds of conditions—which have included two major wars, a considerable amount of industrial unrest, a major inflation and a major depression—Ordinary shares have been able more than to maintain their value in real terms, they must be considered to have met fully the test of soundness. The test applies, however, only if they are considered as a class and only if they have been held over the long term. Many individual shares have suffered severely over the period, while speculatively-minded investors influenced too much by current fashions and by prospects of immediate capital profits and losses, may have been tempted to sell their Ordinary shares only to re-acquire them later at higher prices. In this way they may have lost substantial portions of their capital in the recurrent upward and downward swings in prices.

It would greatly simplify the problems of the investor if he could foresee the future with the same ease with which he can examine the past. The best he can hope to do is to visualize the future in the light of the lessons he has learnt from the past and make such allowances as he can for the ends which society is likely to pursue and the means it is likely to employ in pursuing them. Over the hundred years that we have considered, investment conditions have changed greatly but throughout the period there have been influences at work which remain with us today and continue to influence investment conditions greatly—the recurrence of war and the threat of war, the abhorrence of inflation as a settled way of economic life, the persistence of Capitalism and the profit motive as the main arbiters of our economic destiny and the recurrent threat of trade depressions. If there are important new influences at work they lie in the greatly increased authority of the organized worker and the very much greater emphasis which is now placed on the necessity of assuring to everyone a job. The latter we have seen involves taking risks with money as a store of value, a concept of money which was very dear to our grandfathers.

The future may and no doubt will have many surprises in store for us. As surprises they must however in the nature of things be left out of our calculations. For the present, if we are seeing things in the light of what we have seen we shall place a very much greater emphasis on Ordinary shares in the building up of our investment portfolios than formerly we would have done and we shall balance our Ordinary share portfolios. We will not invest all our Ordinary share fund in one stock which we believe to be outstandingly attractive. If we had done so a generation ago we would probably have chosen, with indifferent results, one of the leading tobacco shares then considered as Ordinary shares to be in the highest class. We shall invest in capitalist enterprise as a whole in such a way that if we have made mistakes in our selection, the effects of these mistakes will be more than taken care of by our successes.

PART IV HOW TO SELECT SECURITIES

CHAPTER XIV

TAXATION AND THE INVESTOR

Income Tax and Yields

The individual's tax position is an important consideration that must always be kept in mind in the selection of securities. Until 1965, British Income Tax was levied on income but not on capital gains. That is to say, if an investor made a profit on the purchase and subsequent sale of a stock, he did not have to pay tax on the profit. On the other hand he did have to pay tax (subject to his liability) on the income, interest or dividend, which he received from the stock while he held it. This had two important consequences. To the investor paying income tax, capital appreciation is more important than an equal amount of income—the higher the rate of tax the more so; while to the investor paying no tax, income and capital appreciation are of equal importance.

Suppose, for example, an investor liable to pay tax at the standard rate is contemplating the purchase of a Government security and has the choice of buying one of two securities —a high-couponed redeemable stock (i.e. one carrying a high rate of interest such as 5% or 5½%) standing at or very close to par or a low-couponed redeemable stock standing well under par, both stocks being in all other respects similar, it will be to his advantage to buy the latter. As we saw earlier the yield on a low-couponed stock with a fixed redemption date and standing under par depends partly on the capital appreciation which is certain to occur by the time the redemption date is reached, whereas the yield on the high-couponed stock if it is standing close to par will depend almost entirely on the current income which it offers, the capital element being negligible. The current income yield on the low-couponed stock, that is the yield on the interest it pays and which is subject to tax, will in the result be lower than the current income yield on the high-couponed stock, most of the difference being made up by the extra capital appreciation exempt from tax, which is in prospect.

2½% Savings Bonds 1964–7 were finally redeemable on 1 May 1967 and 5½% Exchequer Bonds on 15 March 1966. Of the two stocks 2½% Savings Bonds were slightly the longer dated but the difference is not enough to invalidate the conclusions reached from a straightforward comparison of yields. On 27 April 1959, the prices and yields of the two stocks compared as follows:

	Price 27/4/59	Gross Current Yield %	Gross Redemption Yield %	Net Redemption Yield %
2½% Savings Bonds	84 7/16 × d	£2 19 3	£4 17 3	£3 16 0
5½% Exchequer Bonds	103 5/16	5 7 3	5 0 9	2 18 0

(Tax @ 7/9 in the £)

The investor paying tax at the standard rate is not interested in the gross redemption yield since this is a combination of the gross current yield which is subject to tax and the capital profit (or loss as in the case of Exchequer Bonds), which will be secured (or incurred) on the respective redemption dates. What interests him is the net redemption yield. Comparing these he can see at once that the better stock from his point of view, the stock which gives him the best yield after his taxes have been paid, is 2½% Savings Bonds.

The investor who is exempt from income tax will on the other hand look at the gross redemption yields. The gross redemption yield will be wholly gain to him and in view of this he will prefer, of the two stocks, 5½% Exchequer Bonds. In them he will see ahead of him a prospective gross free of tax yield of £5 0s. 9d.% compared with only £4 17s. 3d.% on 2½% Savings Bonds. An additional advantage from his point of view may be that the income will be coming in at once. That is to say, he will not have to wait until the redemption date in eight years to secure the full advantage of his yield.

The investors who are interested in gross yields are not confined to people with small incomes. There are many

TAXATION AND THE INVESTOR

important investing institutions which are exempt from taxes—for example, Pension Funds, Churches, Colleges and Charitable Institutions generally. This does not directly concern the private investor although it does have an important bearing on the prices of securities which private and other investors have to pay—keeping an active interest in securities with high gross redemption yields as the tax-paying investor keeps an active interest in securities with high net redemption yields.

According to the rate of tax he pays (and it is the rate of tax that he pays at the highest end of his income that matters for this purpose), the advantage of low-couponed stocks will vary. If this rate of tax is less than 7s. 9d., say 5s., the advantages will diminish—if more they will increase as follows:

	Net Redemption Yields with Tax.		
	5s. %	7s. 9d. %	10s. %
2¼% Savings Bonds	£4 3 9	£3 16 0	£3 10 0
5½% Exchequer Bonds	3 13 0	2 18 0	2 5 6
Difference	0 10 9	0 18 0	1 4 6

The high surtax payer is therefore even more interested in the low-couponed redeemable stock standing at a heavy discount than the taxpayer who is merely subject to tax at the standard rate.

Low-couponed redeemable stocks standing at a discount best illustrate how a low current yield can sometimes be of advantage to the high taxpayer. There are other cases. The same principles exactly apply, although with more risk, to the Ordinary share or stock which is thought to have exceptional growth possibilities. Such a stock invariably offers a lower yield, occasionally a much lower yield than do Ordinary stocks in general. There is therefore less income to the investor, to attract tax. As the exceptional growth materializes, dividends will in the normal course of events rise, raising the income yield on the original purchase price to a level at least equal to current Ordinary stock yields at the time the purchase was made and probably above them. But in the meantime the price of the stock will also have risen, bringing capital appreciation to the holder and leaving the stock still on a low yield basis compared with existing

Ordinary stocks. The risk is to find the right stock. Not all growth stocks or alleged growth stocks perform as well as they promise. Even so there is still plenty of room for the successful application of this system of selection within the field of Ordinary stocks. There are for example today many companies which are financing their growth by distributing a disproportionately low percentage of their total earnings. Such companies are building up strength for the future when it may be possible to pay much higher dividends. Where this is so, or is thought to be so, the stocks give lower and sometimes much lower dividend yields than their contemporaries. Such stocks are of interest to the surtax payer whereas high yielding Ordinary stocks covered only sparsely by earnings are less likely to be.

Tax considerations should not however be a decisive factor in the selection of individual stocks but they are an important factor which should not be overlooked.

Company Taxes

Until 1965, companies paid income tax on their profits and the profits thus taxed were not again subjected to income tax in the hands of their shareholders when paid to them as dividends. They also paid profits tax on all their income, including investment income. The rate of profits tax although rising was however low. Under the 1965 Finance Act, income tax and profits tax ceased to be assessed on company profits and in their place a new tax, corporation tax, was levied. As in the case of profits tax, the new tax was charged on all income after deducting annual payments such as Loan and Debenture interest from which income tax had been deducted at source. These annual payments were deducted gross.

Although companies ceased to pay income tax on their profits, they were still required to deduct income tax from the interest and dividends they paid. Whereas previously, however, they did not have to account separately to the Inland Revenue for the income tax so deducted (except in special cases where interest was paid, although no profits had been earned or taxable income received), they were now required to do so in all circumstances, under a new tax Schedule—Schedule F. Relief was available only to the extent of tax suffered by deduction from income received e.g. investment income. Such income where it consisted of dividends from other companies which were subject to corporation tax on their profits, was also exempt from corporation tax as "franked investment income".

Although corporation tax was assessed on profits earned before 5th April 1966, it did not come into full operation until after the end of the income tax year 1965/66. As the the following illustration shows, the main effect of the change in the system of taxation introduced by the 1965 Finance Act has been to tax profits, in so far as they are distributed to shareholders, twice—once on the total profits themselves and again on the profits as they are distributed.

		Before 5/4/66		After 5/4/66
Taxable profits		£100,000		£100,000
Less income tax @ 8s. 3d.	£41,125			
profits tax @ 15%	15,000			
		56,125		
corporation tax @ 45%				45,000
		Net £43,875	Gross	£55,000
Less dividend (Gross)		£74,680		£55,000
less tax		30,805		22,687
		£43,875		£32,313

Under the old system of taxation the company, having paid income tax and profits tax, was entitled to pay out in dividends, the remaining profits as fully taxed profits. It was therefore able to pay a gross dividend of £74,680. Under the new system, the maximum gross dividend it can pay is only £55,000. There has, as the result, been a fall of approximately 25% in the profits available for distribution.

When a company declares a dividend it either declares it gross (subject to tax), or net (free of tax). In either event the shareholder may treat the dividend as exempt from further income tax but not from surtax. If the shareholder is for any reason exempt from income tax or is subject to tax at a lower rate than that paid by the company he may recover from the Inland Revenue the income tax deducted from his dividend, to the extent that he has over-paid tax. If on the other hand he is liable to surtax, he must include in his return of income the gross dividend, if it has been declared gross (subject to tax), or the equivalent gross dividend, if it has been declared net (free of tax), and in due course pay surtax at his appropriate rate thereon.

Where dividends are declared free of tax, the equivalent gross dividend is arrived at by calculating what the dividend would have been, which when reduced by tax at the standard rate would have produced the free of tax dividend declared. The method of calculation is as follows, where the tax free dividend is 10% and the standard rate of tax is 7s. 9d. in the £. The dividend paid will be equivalent to 12s. 3d. in the £, i.e. 20s. less 7s. 9d. Therefore the gross dividend will be equivalent to 10% multiplied by 20 and divided by 12¼ or, to get rid of fractions, multiplied by 80 and divided by 49. The answer will be just under 16·3%.

As 16·3% will be the dividend appropriate when calculating gross income for surtax purposes, so it will be the dividend appropriate for calculating relief, if the investor is not subject to income tax. If the investor holds 100 shares of £1 each in a company on which a dividend of 10% tax free has been paid, his gross income from the share will be £16 6s. 6d. Tax at 7s. 9d. in the £ on £16 6s. 6d. will equal £6 6s. 6d., leaving a net dividend of £10, which in fact is what he received. He will therefore be able to claim an appropriately reduced amount, if he is subject to tax at the higher end of his income, at a lower rate than the standard rate.

Tax on Capital Gains

The 1962 Finance Act introduced a tax on short-term gains. These are now taxable as unearned income if they arise from the sale of assets including stocks and shares, purchased within the previous twelve months. Some tangible moveable property, also dwelling houses with grounds of up to an acre, if they are the taxpayer's only or main residence, are exempt from the operation of the tax. Losses may be set off against gains and may be carried forward to later years but they may not be set off against other income. Gains are also taxable where they arise as the result of a bear sale, i.e.

TAXATION AND THE INVESTOR

where the taxpayer sells an asset which he does not possess and at any later date buys it at a lower price.

The 1965 Finance Act extended the tax on short-term gains to long-term gains made on the disposal of assets held for more than twelve months. There are similar exemptions to those applicable to short-term gains with the principal addition of British Government securities, the gains on which remain subject to the short-term gains tax. The rate of tax for private individuals has remained unchanged at 30% since the tax came into operation. Companies, on the other hand, pay the current rate of corporation tax on both their short-term and long-term gains. Private individuals are exempt from tax on the first £50 of their gains in any one year but thereafter they must pay over to the Inland Revenue each additional £1 of gain until the total tax they have paid corresponds again with 30% of the gain, when the flat rate of tax comes again into operation. Where full advantage is to be taken of this relief, it is therefore essential that gains should be kept within the limit of £50. Where it is to their advantage, individuals are assessed on only half the gain, as if it were unearned income, up to a total gain of £5,000 and on the full amount of the excess above that figure. This concession is of advantage where the rate of tax paid by them at the top end of their income, with the proportion of the gain added, does not exceed 12s. in the £.

Where quoted securities are disposed of which were held on 6th April 1965, the seller is entitled when computing his gain to adopt the 6th April value if higher than the original cost. Conversely in computing a loss, he must take the lower of the two values. Where either the original cost or the 6th April 1965 value but not both, exceed the proceeds of sale, there is deemed to be neither a gain nor a loss on disposal. Losses which cannot be set-off against gains in any one year may be carried forward to later years.

Tax and Cum and Ex Dealings

Mention was made earlier in this book about the practice of quoting shares or stock ex dividend (or interest) shortly before the date of payment of the dividend. When shares are quoted ex dividend, the price of the shares is usually reduced by an amount in the region of the net value of the dividend. If the investor is a surtax payer the dividend, after he has paid surtax on it, will be worth less to him than the net amount. If on the other hand he is not liable, even to income tax, the dividend will be worth the gross amount to him less of course any deduction for foreign tax which may have been made and which he may not reclaim.

Arising out of this, it will be in the interest of surtax payers, if they have decided to sell a stock and the quotation of the stock ex dividend is imminent, to sell the stock with as little delay as possible; and conversely if they have decided to buy a stock, to wait in the same circumstances until the stock is quoted ex dividend. For an investor not liable to income tax, the opposite course of action will be advisable. Care should however in both cases be taken to ensure that tax considerations are not being allowed to outweigh in importance investment considerations. A day can make a lot of difference to the fate of a security because within that space of time bad news or good news can intervene to alter completely its investment complexion. If therefore an investor is operating with tax considerations in mind, he should be very sure that he knows the immediate circumstances of the security in which he is dealing and that a sudden change in the investment climate, such as might be associated with a change in Bank Rate, is not immediately probable. He should also bear in mind that surtax can be charged if his income is substantially reduced by avoiding the receipt of dividends or interest in this manner.

CHAPTER XV

THE CHOICE OF INDIVIDUAL SECURITIES

The Investment Background: The Country

As we saw earlier, political and economic conditions sometimes favour one class of security and sometimes another. There are times when circumstances favour Fixed Interest securities (few since the last war) and times when they favour Ordinary shares. We are not however concerned here with the choice between Fixed Interest securities and Ordinary shares, which was dealt with fully in the chapters dealing with investment policy. We are concerned rather with investment conditions as between one country and another, and one industry within a country and another.

First as regards countries, the British investor must start with a very heavy bias in favour of his own country. He has a better understanding of its economics and politics (or should have) than he has of the economics and politics of any other country. Therefore he will incur the extra risks and inconvenience of investment in other countries and in other currencies only if he thinks that by investing in them he will increase the value of his investments and the income he derives from them in terms of sterling. He will bear in mind too that many British companies have interests all over the world and that by purchasing the shares of one of these companies it is possible to cover much wider investment fields than is possible by a purchase of the shares of a British company operating exclusively in the United Kingdom and serving exclusively British customers. There are also many companies which are in only a limited sense United Kingdom companies, but whose shares are actively dealt in on the London market. In these two categories fall the great oil-producing companies, the great soap and margarine combine of Unilever Ltd. and Unilever N.V., the great Rhodesian copper-mining companies, the South African gold and diamond-mining companies and the tea, rubber and tin-mining companies of the Far East.

The British investor is not in fact under a strong compulsion to invest outside the field of securities regularly quoted on the London Stock Exchange in order to maintain a well-balanced portfolio of investments. Yet if he fails to do so he will undoubtedly be missing valuable opportunities. This is particularly true of investment in the United States and in Canada, where political and economic conditions favour the investor to a greater extent than they favour him here. These are richer countries in terms of natural resources. They are still relatively under-populated and they have not yet developed a socialist pattern of thinking which is devoted to the ultimate overthrow of the capitalist system.

In fact in North America the investor should find in the long run more opportunities for increasing his capital than he is likely to find in his own country. He will find the risks greater also because of the greater competition which liberal traditions in these countries have fostered, but he need have no fear of well-chosen investments of high quality made there, especially in the United States, which as earlier mentioned, occupies a dominant position in the economy of the world. The American economy is nearly self-sufficient in terms of raw materials and the country usually has a substantial surplus in its overseas payments. Geographically it is more remote from the main trouble centres of the world.

It is difficult to wax enthusiastic about general investment in other parts of the world. For isolated investments on the other hand there is a case—where for example a certain area is known to be rich in a particularly valuable resource, such as oil in Venezuela. Then the richness of the resource may justify the extra political risks involved in trying to profit from it.

The Industry

The investment background of an industry is generally of less importance than the investment background of a company. There are, however, exceptions. Companies which produce commodities for which the markets are universal are intimately affected by changes in the world prices of these commodities. They are powerless unless they enter into restrictive agreements (which seldom work satisfactorily) to regulate prices and they are unable, however good the managements of particular concerns, to escape their consequences. Companies which fall within this category are, amongst others, those engaged in the production of lead, zinc, copper, tin (the output of which is controlled by international agreement), sugar, pastoral products, shipping (which is of course a service) and oil (the price of which is subject to regulation by the large World producers). Gold-mining companies are also deeply involved in the world price of their product; but in their case, the risk is not of a fall in the selling price of gold, but of a rise in the costs of producing it, resulting from inflation. The price of gold usually remains fixed over long periods of time and is seldom changed, except upwards, as when a country devalues its currency.

With most other industries it is the company rather than the industry that matters and in their cases it is on the company and its record that the investor should focus his main attention. There are, it is true, industries which enjoy growth and industries which do not. The electrical equipment and chemical industries are industries which have for many years enjoyed growth. The motor-car industry and the radio industry are also growing industries, but the same cannot be said of the textile industries in this country with the exception of the branches which are concerned with the manufacture of artificial fibres, such as rayon and nylon. Growth of sales and output and growth of profit do not however necessarily go hand in hand. The rapidly growing industries are also often highly competitive industries. The investor therefore, when selecting the share in which he is to invest, should not be neglectful of the profit record of the industry in which he is investing. He should not as a general rule look for growth in a British cotton share or in a brewing share but he might reasonably expect to find it in a chemical share or an electrical equipment share and perhaps, but not so certainly, in a motor-car or radio equipment share.

The Record of the Company

The profit records of most companies extending back over the past twenty-five years can be easily obtained from one of the statistical services available on company profits. Records extending so far back would normally be of little interest because of important changes which are quite likely to have taken place in company managements in the meantime. Nevertheless records of what happened to companies in the notorious thirties are interesting in showing how much difference the advent of full employment has made to some companies and how comparatively little difference it has made to others. As the investor must always take account of the possibility of investment conditions different from those existing at the time and resembling more closely those which have existed before, knowledge of the past helps him to form an idea of the broad investment standing of the particular share he is thinking of buying.

That said, the years that matter are, say, the last ten. Having made up his mind on the industry, the investor should first compare the profit records of the leading companies in that industry and pay particular regard to the amounts earned on the capital they employ. The amounts earned on the capital they employ is important because companies which have expanded by acquisition of other companies or by amalgamation with other companies may not necessarily have produced better results for their shareholders than companies which have expanded out of their own resources. Out of this comparison one company will emerge more favourably than another. To be fair, however, and to make certain that this company has not emerged well from the comparison merely because the base year for it happened to be a particularly unsuccessful year, or the latest year a particularly successful one, regard should be had to the trend of profits from year to year and to any special circumstances which might have affected the company in its first or last year.

A comparison of dividend policies will also be revealing in reflecting the extent to which shareholders have been allowed to participate in the growth of profits. If a company has persistently followed a conservative dividend policy but dividends have none the less increased satisfactorily, the policy will have justified itself. But if dividends have been kept low and have not been increased in spite of expanding profits, there is reason to question whether the directors of the company have the right attitude towards the shareholders, especially where their own salaries and fees have been rising. Contrariwise, where a conservative dividend policy has been followed and profits have failed to expand, there is reason to question the efficiency of the directors, unless special circumstances have operated in the industry which explain the poor performance.

Profit and dividend records are in fact the only really reliable guides that shareholders have as to the efficiency of the managements of the companies in which they have invested and are thinking of investing. They may know someone who knows the management and believes it to be "first class". But as a general rule this is jargon, more of a snare than a guide to the shareholder who is investing for advantage and not for the fun of it. As the proof of the pudding is in the eating, so the proof of the efficiency of a company's management is in the profits it makes and the dividends it distributes. On performance there is probably no more efficient organization in this country today than Marks and Spencer. It has given its shareholders a princely reward for the faith they have shown in the undertaking. It has expanded out of its own profits and it has given the customer an extremely good service. As the result, the shares are highly valued in relation to current earnings and dividends; but he would be a bold man indeed who claimed that they were in consequence over-valued. They may be highly valued in relation to current earnings and dividends, but to the investor who is looking ahead that is of little account, if, in the light of past performances, there is every reason to expect much larger earnings and dividends in the future.

Knowledge of the quality of a company's management is of great importance, but to be really useful, it should consist of tangible evidence of the benefits likely to accrue to investors if they invest in the company. There are companies which are alleged to be efficiently managed. Yet they have not always been conspicuously successful in rewarding their shareholders.

Financial Strength

More importance has been attached to the financial strength of a company than has usually been justified. The most frequently adopted measure of a company's financial strength is the relationship of its current assets, i.e. cash, debtors and stock, to its current liabilities, i.e. creditors and bank overdraft if any. Financial strength (or weakness) thus assessed is important if the company is making trading losses and little improvement is in sight, for in such circumstances it may be running into serious financial difficulty; but it is of no importance whatever to the company which is and has been trading successfully, except to the extent that it is indicative of a shortage of capital which sooner or later will have to be made good. Such a company when it comes to raise capital is however likely to have no difficulty unless the time when it chooses to raise new capital happens to be a time of general financial stringency. Then it may have to pay more for the new money it raises, if it decides to borrow. In such circumstances however it will be well advised to issue Ordinary shares to existing holders at under the market price of the shares; for then it will be giving nothing away, nor conferring any advantages on Ordinary shareholders who, as the proprietors, do not charge for the money they invest but rely on the investment to yield good profits.

Financial weakness in the sense we have been discussing may in fact be the mark of success and expansion. As a general rule, therefore, it should not be considered apart from the success of the company as a going concern. Where the company is operating successfully, the only respect in which it need be watched is that the prices of the shares of the company may be temporarily weakened, until the new shares that may become available through an issue to raise cash have been absorbed by new permanent investors; for existing investors although they will have the rights to acquire the new shares may prefer not to take them up (they may have no money wherewith to do so), but to sell them. Such a temporary weakening of prices need not concern the long-term investor, although it may justify the new investor pausing a little before he buys.

Lack of financial strength is then not a matter to worry too much about unless the company is already in difficulties for other reasons. On the other side the possession by a company of great financial strength is not by itself a sufficient reason for buying the shares of a company. It may indeed be a reason for questioning the enterprise of the management.

Yield

After profit and dividends the most important consideration is the price of a share or stock. At one price a share may be cheap and attractive in relation to the profit and dividend and at another dear and speculative. The first requirement of a share therefore is that it should give an adequate yield having regard to all circumstances. The difficulty for the investor is to assess all the cirumstances. When he is told that the future lies entirely with atomic energy and that atomic shares are the shares to buy, ought he to discard all the normal methods of assessing values—profits, dividends and yields—and accept as an adequate substitute for them attractive pictures of the shape of things to come? If he is an investor the answer is an emphatic "no". If he would like to have a little speculation and his hunches often come right, well why not? But to confuse that with investment is the way of trouble.

The position is different where he is dealing with the projects of well-established companies who have indicated that they are entering this field and whose records show their managements to be shrewd and business-like. He should be wary, however, about the prices he is asked to pay for the shares. The management makes the profits but the prices of the shares are made by a miscellany of people who may have decided that anything atomic is good to buy and driven the share prices of companies engaged in this branch of activity up to levels which discount good atomic profits for many years to come. The investor, therefore, who follows the "atomic" line, or for that matter any other line that is the current fashion, should attempt to establish how much of a company's business is affected by this activity and how much it already appears to have been allowed for in the price of the shares. He may have difficulty in his researches but a healthy suspicion will serve him in good stead, and even if in the result he may lose a good opportunity now and then, the same suspicion will save him from many losses throughout his investing life. Quite as much money has been lost by investors in high-class over-priced shares, as in second and third-class investments.

Yield is of crucial importance and the investor should insist on getting it; always bearing in mind that it is not just the yield on last year's dividend but the yield on the years to come that matters. How to gauge what the future holds is difficult and he should always be ready to listen to possibilities. They should, however, be possibilities that he understands and that seem in all respects reasonable in the light of what he knows about the company in which he is being advised to invest. And he should not forget that the past tells quite a lot about the future even if it does not tell all.

Yields which are low because the future of a company is held to be very promising are in a different category from yields which are low because of the company's dividend policy. In the one case the investor is being asked to pay for favourable developments that are expected in the future. In the other case the circumstances of the company are already favourable and yields are low merely because instead of paying out larger dividends the company is using the profits withheld for further use in the business. In such a case low yields are much more acceptable, especially where it can be shown that the company has made good use of its profits in the past in expanding its business. In fact the sole justification for conservative dividend policies is that companies hope to make better use for their shareholders of the profits they withhold than the shareholders would be likely to make of them for themselves. If in this they consistently fail (some latitude must be allowed for the normal hazards of business), it is a black mark which justifies the downgrading of the shares to that of a second-class Fixed Interest security. There are some Ordinary shares that fall within this class and they are not generally to be recommended as Ordinary shares. There may be good reasons for the condition in which they find themselves, but often the cause is that the managements have come to regard Ordinary shareholders not as proprietors but as lenders, to be treated as other lenders. Such companies have generally lost their business resilience and have come to be preserves for the managements and their friends rather than enterprises to be developed for their proprietors.

Market Considerations

The investor will want to have some idea of what relationship the price of the share in which he is interested bears to the price of the share in recent years. Is he paying the highest price ever or is he paying a reasonably average price? There are times when it is right to pay a top price if he is buying the shares, but if so he should want to know why he is asked to do so. Conversely if the shares have fallen sharply in price and he is apparently being offered them on bargain terms, he should want to know why the shares have fallen in price. There may be some special reason for the fall, known to people close to the company, which has not yet become public knowledge. These are matters in which his stockbroker ought to be able to guide him but it does not follow that even the stockbroker will always be able to find out the whole truth. Often of course sharp price changes may be the result of general conditions which have affected the prices of all shares. Then it is not so important from the point of view of selection of the individual share although it may be important from the point of view of investment policy generally.

The investor should as a rule concentrate on the better known companies whose shares have a large free market. Because of the wider public interest he will find them easier to buy and easier to dispose of, should he change his mind about their future prospects. He may limit his opportunities as the result, but on the other hand his list of investments should gain in safety. Nor is there any reason why, now and then, he should not make exceptions to this rule.

Fixed Interest Securities

Most of the foregoing considerations apply to Fixed Interest securities as well as to Ordinary shares. The main emphasis however in the case of Fixed Interest securities is on stability. How the capital is secured and how the income is secured is what matters and information on this can be obtained, where the security is a Debenture or a Preference stock, from the same sources that are available on Ordinary shares. The earnings of a company ought to be safe and comfortably more than adequate to meet under all circumstances the interest or dividend requirements of the stock. In addition of course it is important that the yield should be right in relation to yields on comparable stocks.

CHAPTER XVI

THE PROFESSION OF INVESTMENT ADVISING

Advising the Investor

There is much to be learnt about investment, there is much that only experience can teach, but there is also much that can never be known until later when money may have been made or lost. For investment is concerned primarily with what will happen and not with what has happened. No person however expert can know what will happen. He can at best only form an opinion in the light of what he knows about the many influences that are likely to affect the future of securities.

The price of a security at any one time reflects a consensus of opinion based on all that is known about it and the influences which may affect it in the future. This knowledge is partly factual (what is known) and partly non-factual (what is believed).

The investor should endeavour by mastering the theory of investment, which it has been the aim of this book to explain, and by practical experience, to separate the factual from the non-factual. When he has done so and if he has the gift of separating the likely from the unlikely, he should find many opportunities for profitable buying and for wise selling in the course of his investment life. If he has not, and it is a gift partly of imagination and partly of common sense, he will be wise, for the management of his investments, to rely mainly on the guidance of an expert.

To do his job properly, the expert or adviser must know the financial circumstances of the investor. He should at the least know what his total investments are, how they are made up, whether he has any prejudices affecting particular shares and whether he has other sources of income, and if so, how important they are. It is axiomatic that the two should understand and trust one another. Where the fund to be invested is a private trust fund he should of course be aware of the investment powers. In this regard the new Trustee Investments Act has considerably simplified his problems where investments must be confined to Trustee investments. Whereas in such circumstances it was necessary previously to advise resort to the Courts in order to obtain powers to buy Ordinary shares, Trustees now automatically have the power to invest funds under their charge in a wide range of Ordinary shares.

The man ideally equipped for the task in some respects is the stockbroker. He understands markets and has access to all the information which is of importance to the investor. Unfortunately he suffers from one handicap, not fatal but damaging, namely the method by which he is remunerated. He is rewarded not on the basis of his success or failure in handling his client's investments—although of course he may lose a client and sometimes does as the result of bad advice—but on the basis of the shares he buys and sells for his client. If he gives some very good advice to his client as he often does and his client does not act on it, his remuneration is nil for the trouble he has taken. But if his client wants to buy a share or sell a share, based on something he has heard, then the stockbroker gets his commission—perhaps £5, perhaps £100 and perhaps a great deal more, depending on the amount of money involved, without having done much more to earn it than take the order and give it to a jobber.

This inevitably predisposes the broker in favour of making business. He is paid not to look after investments but to buy and sell shares. As the result his chief concern is to produce ideas which lead to business. This is a useful function to perform where he is dealing, as he often is, with large Institutional investors, investment Companies, Unit Trusts, Insurance Companies and Pensions Funds who are capable of assessing the merits of his ideas and who do not look to him to guide them in their investment policies. It can however be positively harmful where he is dealing with private clients, less well equipped to exercise the same judgment and where his gifts of imagination and powers of salesmanship exceed his ability to assess the importance of the many influences which decide the prices of securities. To this latter influence may be attributed many of the exaggerated movements in security prices which have occurred in the past, as well as many of the heavy losses which private speculators and investors have suffered as the result of badly-timed purchases.

The Pursuit of Profits

One of the difficulties that the investment adviser is up against is the unpredictability of short-term movements. While he is weighing up values the prices of the shares he is examining may be rising sharply in price on nothing more substantial than sentiment—the South African uranium shares of a few years ago or the Canadian oil shares of more recent times. He may know that the rises are bogus; but the facts, so far as the client who wants to make profits is concerned, are against him. The price of the shares is rising. The analyst must courageously hold his ground. Only so can he hope to establish his prestige as a sound investment adviser. He may for a time suffer ridicule. He will in due course receive his deserved measure of praise, untinged, let us hope, by remorse over good advice not taken.

To the long-term investor, day to day price movements do not matter if he has confidence in the situation in the long run. They matter only if the price movements are such as to cause him to feel that the security has become too expensive. Rising prices will not then dispose him to buy as they will the speculator but rather to sell on the grounds that the prospect he foresaw has already been fully discounted. Conversely falling prices will dispose him to buy rather than to sell. While some price changes are meaningful and imply a change in a company's investment status, others including usually the most exaggerated ones are not. Where they are not, they may herald merely a new speculative fashion or a new exaggerated fear which the investor should disregard, if it relates to shares in which he has no interest, or turn to his advantage by selling or buying, as the case might be, if it relates to shares in which he has an interest or would like to have an interest.

Where the Investor should go for Advice

The best answer to this question at present is that he should go to his stockbroker, if he has one, or to his bank.

If he is a small investor he may have difficulty in finding a suitable stockbroker, for the basis of remuneration (commission on business done) makes it impossible for the stockbroker to give him the detailed attention he needs. The commissions that his business will yield will be small in relation to the trouble involved in looking properly after his investments. For this reason the small investor is likely, as a general rule, to be better served by his bank who will have the additional interest of being his banker.

Every bank manager however unspecialized in investment can guide the investor's first steps. He can weigh up quickly his client's financial circumstances—whether he or she might be better served by buying a house for his or her own occupation before embarking on the purchase of marketable investments, whether the intending investor has adequately insured his life and whether he has a reasonably secure margin of cash assets to meet any obligation that he may foresee as likely to arise in the future. The bank manager can also explain the risks as well as the advantages of security investment as he can also prescribe the investments likely to be most suitable. For behind every bank manager is an organization and connections with the best available investment opinion. Indeed many bank managers have been trained in the Securities Department of their own bank and are very well equipped through their contacts with stockbrokers to advise both large and small investors on how they should proceed with their investment problems.

For the large investor, and subject to what has been said about the inevitable bias of stockbrokers in favour of making business, the stockbroker, if he is the right one, is almost certainly the best adviser. If the stockbroker is an able and reliable one (and there are very many able and wholly reliable brokers) he will apply exactly the same principles to the handling of his client's investments as he will apply to his own. He will, moreover, have a settled investment policy which he will apply to all his clients. That is to say he will not attempt to deal with every share that has likely possibilities but only with a certain number whose progress he feels able to watch. Whether he will assume full responsibility for managing his client's investments or whether he will accept the responsibility only on an advisory basis, will be a matter for arrangement between himself and his client. In general the client will be wise to keep the main responsibility in his own hands. It is true that, in that case, there will be the risk of divided responsibility; but the risk is unlikely to be a serious one if the relations between the broker and his client are easy relations based on mutual trust and confidence.

Apart from stockbrokers and the investment departments of banks, a number of professional advisers exist who are fully competent to give the best advice that brokers can give. They are less easy to find however and great care is needed in their selection. In general, modern capitalist society, in which the investor is for the most part separate from the management, has failed so far to evolve the proper investment service for the investor—Investment Trust Companies (and in their small way, Unit Trusts) are an oblique response, but cannot nearly cover the whole ground, so far as one can see.

APPENDIX I

INDEX TO THE STOCK EXCHANGE DAILY OFFICIAL LIST

Banks and Discount Companies.
Breweries and Distilleries.
British Funds, etc.
Canals and Docks.
Commercial, Industrial, etc.
Corporation and County Stocks—Great Britain and Northern Ireland.
Corporation Stocks—Dominion and Colonial.
Corporation Stocks—Foreign.
Dominion, Provincial and Colonial Government Securities.
Electric Lighting and Power.
Financial Trusts, Land, etc.
Foreign Stocks, Bonds, etc.
Gas.
Insurance.
Investment Trusts.
Unit Trusts.
Iron, Coal and Steel.
Mines.
Nitrate.
Oil.
Property.
Public Boards, etc.
Railways.
Rubber.
Shipping.
Tea and Coffee.
Telegraphs and Telephones.
Trade Facilities and other Acts Securities.
Tramways and Omnibus.
Waterworks.

APPENDIX II
BUYING AND SELLING CONTRACT NOTES

Buying

```
X.Y. & COMPANY                              Address
   Partners.                         20th October, 1961.

   BOUGHT by order of P.Q.R. subject to the Rules and
   Regulations of the Stock Exchange.

   200 Shares of 5/– each in The Delta
       Metal Company Limited at 20/– xd    £200   0   0
       Transfer Stamp and Fee   £2   2   6
       Contract Stamp                2   0
       Commission               2   10   0       4  14   6
                                              _____
       Total cost                             £204  14   6

                              X.Y. & COMPANY
For Settlement                      2/–
   7th November, 1961.         Contract Stamp
                           Members of the Stock Exchange
E. & O.E.                         London.
```

Selling

```
X.Y. & COMPANY                              Address
   Partners                          20th October, 1961.

   SOLD by order of P.Q.R. subject to the Rules and Regu-
   lations of the Stock Exchange.

   £50 Ordinary Stock in Liebig's Extract
       of Meat Company Limited @ 19/9
       per unit of 5/– each                £197  10   0
       Contract Stamp          £0   2   0
       Commission               1   4   8         1   6   8
                                              _____
       Total proceeds                         £196   3   4

                              X.Y. & COMPANY
For Settlement                      2/–
   7th November, 1961.         Contract Stamp
                           Members of the Stock Exchange
E. & O.E.                         London.
```

NOTES:

(1) The London Stock Exchange year is divided into 20 Accounts of 2 weeks each and 4 of 3 weeks each. The four 3-week accounts cover the main holiday periods—Christmas, Easter, Whitsun and the Summer Bank Holiday. Dealings for an Account begin on a Monday and end on the Friday of the following week or of the second following week, if a three week Account, and are settled on the second Tuesday after the end of dealings. Dealings for the Account to which the above transactions related began on Monday, 16 October 1961 and ended on Friday, 27 October 1961. The settlement date was consequently Tuesday, 7 November 1961.

The arrangement is of concern mainly to brokers in their dealings with jobbers. How clients settle with their brokers is a matter between them and their brokers. Government securities are dealt in for cash. The settlement for them is not therefore affected by the Account days.

(2) A reduced commission was charged in the case of the sale. The full commission would have been £2 9s. 4d. but as the transactions involved a purchase and a sale by the same person, Stock Exchange rules permit the charging of a reduced commission at half the normal rate in the case of the transaction involving the smaller full commission, in this case the selling transaction.

(3) The shares of The Delta Metal Company Limited were bought xd. This means that the dividend when paid will be retained by the seller.

APPENDIX III

SCALE OF MINIMUM COMMISSIONS

A. (1)

British Government Securities
British Electricity Guaranteed Stocks
British Gas Guaranteed Stocks
British Transport Guaranteed Stocks
Securities guaranteed under the Trade Facilities and other Acts
Indian Government Stocks
London County Consolidated Stocks
†Dominion and Colonial Government Securities
†County, Corporation and Provincial Securities (British, Dominion or Colonial)
Public Boards (Great Britain and Northern Ireland) Inscribed and Registered Stocks
International Bank for Reconstruction and Development Stock

} ⅜ per cent. on Stock up to £10,000 Stock. ¼ per cent. on Stock on any balance in excess of £10,000 Stock.

†See also A. (2) below.

A. (2)
(i) Dominion and Colonial Government, Provincial, County and Corporation Securities
    Bonds to Bearer either expressed in a currency other than Sterling or carrying an option for payment at a fixed rate in a currency other than Sterling, where the price is over 100
(ii) County, Corporation and Provincial Securities (British, Dominion or Colonial)
    Annuities (dealt in per unit of Annuity)
(iii) Bank of Ireland Stock

} ⅜ per cent. on money.

B.

Debentures and Bonds (Registered or Bearer) and any other securities representing loans (Loan Stocks, Notes etc.), other than those included in Section A . . . . . ¼ per cent. on consideration.

C.

Registered Stocks (quoted per cent.) other than those included in Section A or B . 1¼ per cent. on consideration.

D.

Shares or Units of Stock, Registered or Bearer (other than Shares included in Section E)　　1¼ per cent. on consideration.

E.

Shares of Companies incorporated in the United States of America or Canada (whether dealt in in London on a Dollar or Sterling basis), with the exception of Shares which are transferable by Deed of Transfer.

The Dollar prices set out in the scale below relate to transactions done for settlement in Sterling (including any premium paid or received).

For the purpose of applying the scale to transactions effected in overseas markets where payment is made and received in Dollars, the American or Canadian Dollar price is to be converted into the Sterling equivalent at the current rate of exchange.

Price 25 cents (1/) or under . . . . . At discretion.

Price

					s.	d.	
Over 25 cents	(1/)	to 37½ cents	(1/6)		0	0¼	per Share
,, 37½ ,,	(1/6)	to 62½ ,,	(2/6)		0	0½	,,
,, 62½ ,,	(2/6)	to 87½ ,,	(3/6)		0	0¾	,,
,, 87½ ,,	(3/6)	to $1¼	(5/)		0	1	,,
,, $1¼	(5/)	to $2½	(10/)		0	1½	,,
,, $2½	(10/)	to $3¾	(15/)		0	2¼	,,
,, $3¾	(15/)	to $5	(£1)		0	3	,,
,, $5	(£1)	to $7½	(£1/10/)		0	3¾	,,
,, $7½	(£1/10/)	to $10	(£2)		0	4½	,,
,, $10	(£2)	to $12½	(£2/10/)		0	6	,,
,, $12½	(£2/10/)	to $15	(£3)		0	7½	,,
,, $15	(£3)	to $20	(£4)		0	9	,,
,, $20	(£4)	to $25	(£5)		1	0	,,
,, $25	(£5)	to $37½	(£7/10/)		1	3	,,
,, $37½	(£7/10/)	to $50	(£10)		1	6	,,
,, $50	(£10)	to $75	(£15)		1	9	,,
,, $75	(£15)	to $100	(£20)		2	0	,,
,, $100	(£20)	to $150	(£30)		2	3	,,
,, $150	(£30)	to $200	(£40)		2	6	,,

With an increase of 6d. for every $50, or portion thereof, in price.

APPENDIX IV

HOW TO CALCULATE YIELDS

When calculating yields the two things that have to be established are the price or capital value and the income. When these are known the result can be simply arrived at by dividing the income by the price and multiplying the result by 100; this, of course, expresses the income as a percentage of the price. In the case of Fixed Interest securities the calculation is normally based on £100 of stock. (Government securities and Debentures, that is to say; but not Preference stocks which are most usually dealt in units of £1.) The income is determined by the rate of interest the stock pays, £4 10s. 0d. if the stock pays 4½% and £5 if the stock pays 5%. The price is the price the buyer pays or the seller receives plus the expenses incurred in making the purchase, if it is a purchase and less the expenses suffered in effecting the sale, if it is a sale (see page 38 of Chapter IV).

The principles are the same for calculating the yield on Ordinary shares except that the unit is seldom £100, most usually £1 and frequently less than £1. The income is the latest dividend for a full year that has been paid on the Ordinary shares, expressed in terms of one Ordinary share. For example a dividend of 20% on a share with a nominal value of 5s. would be 1s. while the same rate of dividend on a share with a nominal value of £1 would be 4s. Where a company pays interim and final dividends and there has been a change in the interim dividend since the last full year's dividend was paid, which implies a future change in the total dividend, this information should be noted but not used for the purpose of calculating the income of the stock, for without the knowledge of the final dividend it is impossible to say what the total new dividend will be.

Prices should be adjusted (see page 37) in the case of Fixed Interest securities to allow for interest or dividend accumulated in the price but not in the case of Ordinary shares unless the dividend has been declared and the shares are quoted cum the dividend. The distinction is not logical but can be defended on the grounds that Ordinary dividends are not known until they are declared and that to disregard accumulated dividends gives a more conservative result to a buyer. Where adjustments are made to the price in respect of interest and dividends, the adjustments for the individual investor should be made gross or net after the deduction of tax, depending on the investor's tax position. That is to say if the investor is liable to pay tax at the standard rate on his investment income, interest and dividend income will be worth no more than its net value to him, and even less if he pays surtax. If on the other hand he is exempt from income tax, interest and dividend income will be worth its gross value to him. When calculating yields without regard to any particular individual investor it is usual to assume that investors will be liable at least to the full standard rate of tax and accordingly adjustments for interest and dividends are made net after the deduction of tax.

(a) Fixed Interest Securities.

Purchase price of £100 3½% 1st Perpetual Debenture Stock Watney Mann Limited
20 October 1961   £50·000
  Add: Transfer Stamp   ·500
     Commission   ·375
                 £50·875
  Less: Accrued interest net from 5/10/61
     until 20/10/61   ·056

Total cost including expenses and after deducting accrued interest   £50·819

Income from stock—£3 10 0 or

$$\therefore \text{Yield} = \frac{3\cdot 5 \times 100\%}{50\cdot 819} = 6\cdot 887 \text{ or } £6 \;\; 17 \;\; 9\%.$$

NOTES:

(1) The price taken for purchase is the offered price (the higher) and for sales the bid price (the lower).
(2) The principles for calculating the yield on a Government security will be the same except that there will be no charge for transfer stamp.
(3) If the transaction were a sale, expenses would be deducted from the proceeds and there would be no charge for transfer stamp.
(4) The small charge for the contract stamp in this case 1s. is disregarded.
(5) Had the stock been ex interest at the time when the purchase was made, the net interest still to accrue until the interest date would have to be added to the price. The

reason for this is that once the stock is quoted ex interest, it ceases to earn interest for a buyer until the next interest period begins. This sacrifice of interest is part of the price the buyer is paying for the stock. The seller who receives the interest is in a like fashion receiving in effect more for his stock than the selling price.

(b) Ordinary Shares.

Purchase price of one 5s. Share of The Delta Metal Company Limited   20/– xd. =   £1·0000
Add: Transfer Stamp   0·0100
Commission   0·0125

Total cost including expenses   £1·0225

Income from stock from dividend of 20% = 1s. or £0·05

$$\therefore \text{Yield} = \frac{0\cdot05 \times 100}{1\cdot0225} = \frac{5\cdot0}{1\cdot0225} = 4\cdot89\% \text{ or } £4\ 17\ 9\%.$$

NOTES:

(1) As in the case of Fixed Interest securities, expenses will be deducted where the transaction is a sale and there will be no charge for transfer stamp. The prices used will also be "offered" for a purchase and "bid" for a sale.

(2) If the share had been a bearer share there would have been no charge for transfer stamp provided it was in stamped form.

APPENDIX V

GOVERNMENT CONTROL OF INTEREST RATES

Before describing the methods of control it might be useful to say a little about the circumstances in which the control operates. First, inflation implies a heavy demand for the use of money. If this demand is met by a readiness to create more and more money, inflation will get worse but interest rates may not rise. If on the other hand the demand is resisted by a decision to keep the supply of money constant, then interest rates will rise as the only effective means of rationing the limited supply. Secondly, action on the supply of money is not the only way of dealing with the problem of inflation. Action can also be taken through the Budget. The Government can reduce the amount of income the public has to spend by increasing taxation, or it can reduce its own expenditures. If it increases taxes enough or reduces its expenditures enough, the threat of inflation may be abolished without the need for any action on the supply of money. The way may then be paved for an easy money policy and a lower level of interest rates in order to revive the economy. Thirdly, the appropriateness of action through the supply of money, or alternatively through the Budget will tend to be decided (*a*) by the speed with which action is needed and (*b*) by whether the remedy should be found by action on consumption or on investment. Monetary action is the speedier action but exerts its influence mainly on the levels of new saving and new investment. Budgetary action is the slower action but exerts its main influence on the level of consumption.

Consistent with the foregoing it would be true to say that as a general rule inflation forces interest rates upwards because it makes borrowers ready to pay higher rates and because it leads to action which causes lenders to have less than enough to meet all demands made upon them, while deflation forces interest rates downwards because lenders have more than enough money to meet existing demands and are encouraged in consequence to lower their charges to borrowers in the hope of creating new demands.

A great deal of time could be unprofitably spent on arguing whether the Government controls the rate of interest or whether

APPENDIX V

it is decided by economic forces beyond the control of the Government. The facts are however that the Government controls, through the Bank of England, the supply of money, and by having made itself responsible for the general health of the economy also plays a decisive part in regulating the total demand for money. Its control is however general not particular. It does not decide what rate of interest is to be charged by A to B for a loan. It merely controls the climate in which they come to terms and it does it in several ways. It consumes approximately one-third of the gross national product and it decides how much of this is to be paid for by people out of taxes and how much of it is to be paid for by borrowing. It decides the Bank Rate and it decides in general how much money the banks are to have to lend, whether their total loans and investments are to be in the region of £4,500 million as they are now or whether they are to be in the region of £1,500 million as they were before the war. The mechanism works in the following way.

The Bank of England controls the credit base. The credit base consists of the aggregate cash reserves of the clearing banks. These cash reserves are made up of two parts—Bank of England notes and coins which the clearing banks hold in their tills to meet the day to day demands of their customers for ready money and their balances with the Bank of England, on which they are free to draw at any time. By convention, which is strictly adhered to, the clearing banks must maintain minimum cash reserves equal to 8% of the total sums of money which members of the public have deposited with them. If their cash reserves fall below 8%, they must reduce their loans or sell some of their investments in order to acquire cash and if their cash reserves rise above 8% they are free to increase their loans or add to their investments.

The size of their cash reserves in the aggregate is decided by the Bank of England. If the Bank of England wants the banks to lend more money it can buy securities. It can buy securities in the ordinary way that a private investor buys securities, or it can buy or take over securities from the Government.

In either event it creates a claim upon itself which sooner or later finds its way into the hands of the clearing banks. If the banks have not been losing cash to the public, as has happened in recent years, through a rise in the public's demands for ready money, their cash reserves will rise by this amount. With more cash in hand they will be able to lend more and invest more. The additional amount that they have to lend and invest will not however be limited to the extra amount of cash but will extend to a multiple of $12\frac{1}{2}$ times that amount. For example if £8 is the appropriate cash reserve against every £100 of deposits and the cash reserve is increased to £9, then it will be possible for deposits to increase to £112 10s. 0d. before the minimum cash reserve of 8% is again reached.

The increase will not take place suddenly but will occur gradually spreading from one bank to another. When a bank grants a loan or makes an investment it creates a deposit. The new deposit may be with one of its own customers in which event it will not lose cash to another bank but it may also be with one of the customers of another bank in which event it will lose cash. The other bank will however now be in a position to extend its business and in the process create new deposits. So gradually in time, if the addition to cash reserves is permanent the level of total deposits, total loans and total investments will settle at a level appropriate to the new level of cash reserves.

The converse will be true if the Bank of England decides to reduce cash reserves.

Because the Government has been a large borrower in recent years and because it relies on the banking system to provide its needs initially against the issue of Treasury Bills, the control over the supply of money exercised by the Bank of England has in practice been less effective than it might have been. The reason has been the Bank's wish to keep the rate of interest on Treasury Bills fairly stable. To do this it has been prepared to buy Treasury Bills freely, thereby making them virtually as liquid as cash. The result has been to weaken greatly the influence of cash as the sole instrument of credit control.

The Bank's reason for wishing to maintain a fairly stable Treasury Bill rate has been its belief that thereby the Government will be able to fund more and more of its short-term debt into longer-term debt. As the funding of short-term debt is in turn only required because of the ease with which Treasury Bills can be turned into cash, the remedy may lie in the suspension of funding operations during periods when the Government, for economic reasons, wishes to keep the supply of money tight. Such a suspension would have the additional advantage of avoiding the need for the Government to borrow long term when conditions are least favourable, from the Government's point of view, to such an operation.

APPENDIX VI

YIELDS ON REDEEMABLE SECURITIES

Redemption yields are made up of two components—the current income yield and the capital profit or loss yield. The two are combined to make one gross yield or one net yield (after deducting tax from the interest payments) to redemption. The main difficulty in calculating the yield (and it is work for an actuary unless tables are used), is that the capital profit or loss has to be expressed as so much per annum and before this can be done it is necessary to know what rate of interest to use. A capital profit of say £10 receivable in 5 years is worth less than £2 per annum payable for 5 years, for it will be possible to invest each £2 at a rate of interest to produce a greater sum than £10 at the end of 5 years. The rate of interest that should be used is the same rate of interest as the rate of interest or yield that is being calculated. As that is not known it has to be estimated until, by trial and error, a rate is found which produces an equation between the price of the stock on the one hand and the present values of the future interest payments until redemption of the stock and of the capital sum that will be payable on redemption on the other. The methods are the same whether a gross or a net redemption yield is being calculated except that in the case of a net redemption yield, tax is deducted from the annual interest payments.

The present value of a sum payable in the future is the value now before the addition of the interest that will be earned to make up the sum. For example the present value of 105 payable in one year is 100 assuming the rate of interest to be 5%. With this in mind the gross redemption yield (or net redemption yield) may be explained by the following illustration. A security pays 3% per annum, it is redeemable in three years and its present price is £95. The buyer of the security, in return for the £95 he pays, will receive three annual interest payments of £3 and a capital sum of £100 in three years. The gross redemption rate of interest is the rate which gives a total present value of exactly £95 for the aggregate of the three interest payments and the capital sum of £100. Put another way it is the rate of interest which when added annually to the sum of £95, less the three annual payments of interest as they fall due, produces exactly £100 in three years.

APPENDIX

THE DELTA METAL COMPANY LIMITED
DATED BALANCE SHEET—

1956 £	£		£	£
	2,000,000	SHARE CAPITAL OF HOLDING COMPANY: Authorized: 16,000,000 Shares of 5s. each	4,000,000	
2,000,000		Issued: 11,660,000 Shares of 5s. each		2,915,000
1,538,239	1,538,239 —	CAPITAL RESERVES: Share Premium Account Fixed Assets Reserve	4,331,312 1,104,658	5,435,970
	2,182,577 436,385 110,046	REVENUE RESERVES AND UNDISTRIBUTED PROFITS: General Reserves Pension and Profit-sharing Reserves Reserves on Book Debts Profit and Loss Appropriation	2,482,577 436,385 110,046	
2,947,240	218,232	Account Balances	238,272	3,267,275
6,485,479				11,618,250
878,700		FUTURE TAXATION: Income Tax 1958/9		658,073
	216,326	SHARE INTEREST AND LOAN CAPITAL IN SUBSIDIARY COMPANIES HELD OUTSIDE THE GROUP: Preference Shares Ordinary Shares (including proportion of undistributed	432,673	
473,820	32,494 25,000 200,000	profits attributable thereto) Debentures Unsecured Notes	33,824 24,705 200,000	691,202
	57,757 2,421,479 1,078,417	CURRENT LIABILITIES: Canadian Subsidiary's Bank Overdraft (secured) Creditors and Provisions Taxation accrued to date Proposed Final Dividend and Bonus for the year ended	35,530 1,232,490 1,466,542	
3,787,653	230,000	31 December, 1957 (net)	310,150	5,050,812
11,625,652				£18,018,337

W. E. OGDEN } Directors
W. W. DOLTON }

VII

AND SUBSIDIARY COMPANIES CONSOLI-
31st DECEMBER, 1957

1956				
£	£		£	£
		FIXED ASSETS:		
		FREEHOLD AND LEASEHOLD PREMISES:		
	3,597,690	As professionally valued at 31 December, 1956	5,961,615	
	53,880	At net book value at 1 July, 1948, or at cost	471,868	
	3,651,570		6,433,483	
3,648,991	2,579	Depreciation written off since	106,514	6,326,969
		PLANT AND MACHINERY AND EQUIPMENT:		
	346,094	Balance at 1 January, 1948 less sales	710,469	
	2,145,586	Net Additions since (at cost)	4,488,245	
	2,491,680		5,198,714	
1,479,744	1,011,936	Depreciation written off since	2,425,986	2,772,728
5,128,735				9,099,697
		INVESTMENTS, AT COST LESS PROVISIONS:		
	126,779	Quoted Securities	99,290	
	110,821	Unquoted Securities	324,360	
687,491	449,891	Debentures and Secured Loans	388,638	812,288
		CURRENT ASSETS:		
	2,034,615	Stocks, as valued by Managing Directors	3,310,496	
	2,374,974	Debtors and Payments in Advance	3,616,135	
	230,000	Tax Reserve Certificates	120,050	
5,809,426	1,169,837	Cash at Bank and on Short Loan	1,059,671	8,106,352
11,625,652				£18,018,337

From the shareholder's point of view this is one of the better ways of presenting a conventional Balance Sheet. The Assets are clearly set forth and also the Liabilities, as well as the aggregate figure of Capital and Reserves. While the Share Capital consists of 11,660,000 shares of 5s. each, having a total value of only £2,915,000, the actual capital employed by the company is £11,618,250 which divided amongst the 11,660,000 shares gives a value per share not of 5s. but of 19s. 11d.

An alternative way of presenting the main headings of the Balance Sheet which highlights the shareholder's interest would be:

1956			1957	
£	£	ASSETS:	£	£
	3,648,991	FREEHOLD AND LEASEHOLD PREMISES		6,326,969
	1,479,744	PLANT, MACHINERY AND EQUIPMENT		2,772,728
	687,491	INVESTMENTS AT COST, LESS PROVISIONS		812,288
	5,809,426	CURRENT ASSETS		8,106,352
	11,625,652	TOTAL ASSETS		18,018,337
		LESS LIABILITIES:		
878,700		FUTURE TAXATION	658,073	
473,820		SHARE INTEREST AND LOAN CAPITAL IN SUBSIDIARY COMPANIES HELD OUTSIDE THE GROUP*	691,202	
3,787,653		CURRENT LIABILITIES	5,050,812	
	5,140,173	TOTAL LIABILITIES		6,400,087
	6,485,479	SHAREHOLDERS' FUNDS		11,618,250
		Made up as follows:		
		SHARE CAPITAL OF HOLDING COMPANY:		
2,000,000		Authorized	4,000,000	
		Issued:		
	2,000,000	11,660,000 Shares of 5s. each		2,915,000
	1,538,239	CAPITAL RESERVES		5,435,970
	2,947,240	REVENUE RESERVES		3,267,280
	£6,485,479			£11,618,250

* Where a company whose accounts are being consolidated (the parent company) owns less than the total Ordinary share capital of its subsidiary company or companies (the company or companies in which it has a controlling interest), the assets and liabilities of the subsidiary company or companies must be apportioned, for the purpose of the Consolidated Balance Sheet, between the parent company and the outside shareholders. The resulting net assets (that is assets less liabilities) representing the apportioned share of the outside shareholders, plus any liabilities to outside shareholders of subsidiary companies in respect of Preference Debenture and Loan capital, must appear as a liability in the parent company's Balance Sheet, as they represent assets which do not belong to the parent company.

APPENDIX VIII

PROFIT AND LOSS ACCOUNT AND PRIORITY PERCENTAGES

The Delta Metal Company Limited and Subsidiary Companies Year Ended 13st December 1957

Consolidated Profit and Loss Account

1956 £	1956 £		1957 £	1957 £
1,901,727		Group Trading Profit		1,858,714
142,085		*Add:* Dividends and Interest received (less paid)		87,139
	2,043,812			1,945,853
212,755		*Deduct:* Depreciation of Fixed Assets	330,959	
77,936		Management Remuneration	81,787	
	290,691			412,746
	1,753,121	Group Profit, before Taxation		1,533,107
220,809		*Deduct:* Profits Tax	248,150	
735,691		Income Tax	452,200	
	956,500			700,350
	796,621	Group Net Profit, after Taxation		832,757
	421	*Deduct:* Proportion of net profit attributable to Shares in Subsidiary Companies held outside the Group		11,467
	796,200	Profit attributable to Holding Company		821,290
	45,608	*Deduct:* Profits retained in Subsidiary Companies' Accounts		13,238
	750,592	Balance of Profit dealt with in Holding Company's Accounts		868,052

177

Appropriation Account

1956 £	£		£	£
750,592		Balance of Profit brought into Holding Company's Account		808,052
81,759		Add: Amount brought forward from previous year		82,351
832,351		Balance Available for Distribution by Holding Company:		890,403
		Deduct: Appropriations for the year:		
400,000		General Reserve	300,000	
—		Research and Development	50,000	
15,000		Employees' Welfare and Benefit Fund	20,000	
105,000		Interim Dividend of 10% (less tax) on £2,000,000	115,000	
230,000	750,000	Final Dividend of 15% and Bonus of 5% (both less tax) on £2,750,000	316,250	801,250
82,351		Balance carried forward, per Holding Company's Balance Sheet		89,153
135,881		Add: Balance of Profit carried forward by Subsidiary Companies (including £135,881 from previous year)		149,119
218,232		TOTAL UNDISTRIBUTED PROFITS, PER CONSOLIDATED BALANCE SHEET		238,272

NOTE: The Interim and Final Dividends paid for 1956 were paid on a lower outstanding amount of Ordinary Share capital than the interim and Final Dividends paid for 1957.

APPENDIX VIII

From these two accounts it can be gleaned that the profits of the group as a whole for the Year ended 31 December 1957 were £821,290. Profits retained in Subsidiary Companies' Accounts are a deduction from the Holding Company profits but not from the profits of the Group as a whole which belong to the shareholders of the Delta Metal Co. Nor are profits brought forward from the previous year an addition to profits of the current year although they must be added, as the company has done, to produce the final figure which will be carried forward to the next year and which is shown in the Balance Sheet as part of the total of Revenue Reserves:

We have then a Consolidated Profit of		£821,290
From this should be deducted—		
Appropriation for Research and Development	£50,000	
Employees' Welfare and Benefit Fund	20,000	70,000
Leaving as available for Ordinary Shareholders' dividends and reserves		751,290
The Cost of the 30% dividend which the Company paid out of these profits was		431,250

And as there is no Senior Capital of the parent Company ranking ahead of the Ordinary Capital the priority percentages can be quite simply calculated as follows:—

	% of Profits
Ordinary Dividends	0– 57·4
Reserves	57·4–100·0

It is necessary at this stage to enter one important reservation. The company paid a 30% dividend during the year but it was not paid on the full amount of Ordinary Share Capital outstanding at the end of the year. As the result of this the figure of £431,250 understates the cost of the dividend on the present capital by approximately £70,000. On the other hand the capital was increased by the absorption of two other companies, the profits of one of which were included in the companies' profits to the extent of only three months and the profits of the other of which were completely ignored. It would not therefore be right to include the cost of the dividend on the capital as increased without at the same time including the full profits of the two companies which were absorbed. As these have not been disclosed by the company, the statement of priority percentages with its admitted limitations is the best that the shareholder can hope to achieve. The true position may be better and it may be worse than the figures suggest but it is not likely to be very greatly different.

One final point remains to be underlined. The 30% dividend paid by the company will relate in future, if it is repeated, to an issued capital of £2,915,000. As we saw from a study of the Consolidated Balance Sheet, the total value of the capital employed by the company is £11,618,250. If the dividend was expressed in terms of this figure the rate of dividend would be not 30% but almost exactly 7½%.

INDEX

Australian Securities, 97, 98

Balance Sheet, 33, 67, 71, 72, 174, 175, 176
Bank Deposits, 22
Building Society Deposits, 21, 22
 Shares, 22, 135

Canadian Securities, 96, 148
Capital Employed, 72, 73, 150
Capital Gains Tax, 50, 51, 57, 123, 145, 146
Commission, 29, 31, 32, 158, 160, 165, 166
Commonwealth, and Colonial, Government Securities, 57, 58
Corporation Tax, 64, 74, 105, 142, 143

Debenture Stocks, 10, 60, 61, 62, 74, 155
 Convertible, 63, 70, 71
Defence Bonds, 20, 21
Double Taxation Relief, 93

Endowment Assurance Policies, 16, 17

Fixed Interest Securities
 and Inflation, 45, 54, 117, 122, 123, 124, 125, 131, 132
 and Interest Rates, 36, 38, 39, 51, 52, 53, 115, 116, 117
 Merits of, 27, 132, 133, 134
 Nature of, 25, 27, 47
 and Taxation, 139, 140, 141
 Yield of, 36, 53, 54, 167, 168

Gearing, 75, 103, 104, 105, 109
Government Securities, 33, 47, 48, 49, 56, 57

Industrial Grants, 73

Interest Rates
 Changes in, 39, 40, 41, 45, 116, 117, 118, 123, 170, 171, 172
 Influence on Security Prices, 36, 38, 39, 51, 52, 53, 115, 116, 117
Investment Companies, 101, 102, 103, 104, 105, 109, 161

Life Annuities, 14, 15
 Assurance Policies, 14, 15, 16, 19
Loan Stocks, 60, 61, 62
Local Authority Stocks, 58, 59, 60

Marketable Securities
 Dealing in, 29, 30, 31, 32
 Information, 33, 34
 Income, 32, 33
 Merits of, 34, 35
 Nature of, 24, 25, 26, 27, 28, 29
 Yield of, 36, 38, 39

National Savings Certificates, 20

Ordinary Shares
 Asset Values, 82, 83, 84
 Calculation of Earnings, 74, 75, 179
 Classes of Shares, 84, 85, 86, 87, 88, 89, 90
 Inflation, 45, 76, 122, 123, 124, 125, 132
 Interest Rates, 115, 116, 117
 Merits of, 10, 27, 45, 135, 136, 137
 Nature of, 10, 25, 32, 33, 66
 Nominal or par values, 67, 68
 Price fluctuations, 108, 111, 112, 120, 121, 137, 155, 159
 Rights issues, 69, 70
 Risks of, 10, 77, 108, 134

INDEX

Ordinary Shares (*continued*)
    Spread of, 102, 106, 107, 108, 109, 136, 137
    Taxation and, 141, 142, 143, 145
    Yields of, 75, 76, 141, 142, 153, 154, 167, 168, 169

Pensions
    National Insurance, 17
    Retirement, 17, 18, 19
Post Office Savings Bank Deposits, 20, 21, 25
Preference Shares, 10, 63, 64, 155
Premium Savings Bonds, 20, 21
Price-earnings Ratio, 74, 75, 94
Priority Percentages, 74, 75
Profit and Loss Account, 71, 73, 177, 178, 179
Property, 22, 23, 24
    Mortgages, 24

Redeemable Securities, 10, 38, 39, 48, 49, 50, 51, 52, 53, 132, 133, 173
Rhodesian Securities, 100

Share Capital, 33, 66, 67, 72
South African Securities, 98, 99, 100

Take-over bids, 83, 84
Tax Reserve Certificates, 21
Trustee Investments, 132, 134, 135, 158
    Savings Bank Deposits, 20, 21

Unit Trusts, 29, 101, 102, 106, 107, 108, 109, 110, 135, 161
United States Securities, 91, 92, 93, 94, 95, 127, 128, 144, 148

Yields, Calculation of, 36, 37, 38, 167, 168, 169